Slobodan Radojev Mitric, also known as Karate Bob, is a former top Yugoslav Counter Intelligence agent who, after defecting to the West in 1973, in 1993 succeeded former CIA director for Asia and Europe, Major-General Raymond Healey, as World Director of Reserve Police International (RPI), an organization at that time based in Tucson. A Karate master 10th Dan and criminologist with an honorary degree in law from the Arizona College of Police Science (1986), he is also a poet, playwright and artist in his own right.

The cover of his book shows the mirrored title page of the screen-play entitled *Operation Twins* by the author dated in 1982. It was also used for the cover of part 1 of the republished English book version from 2005.

The author lives and works in exile from his native country Serbia since 1973 in Amsterdam under constant threat of being depo rted and has not appeared in public since June 2010. He was married to the Dutch artist Iris de Vries, who died on January 10, 2006 under suspicious circumstances in an Amsterdam hospital. See his docu-mented CV in the appendices.

By Slobodan Radojev Mitric

In English

Operation Twins (Part 1, 2005)
Operation Twins (Excerpt, Part 2, 2006)
The Golden Tip – The Entanglement of the Upper and
Underworld and the Murder of Gerrit Jan Heijn (2009)
Help! They've Kidnapped Me! Lady Di (2010)
The Battle of Kosovo (2011)
World Mythology – Bible of the Man Without Faith (2011)

Pending

Confessions of a Disgruntled Spy

In Dutch

Het Grote Karateboek (1981)
Geheim Agent van Tito (1981)
Tito's Moordmachine ((1982)
Bijbel van de man zonder geloof (1984)
Nederland's maffia (1985)
De slag bij Kosovo (1989)
De Gouden Tip – De verstrengeling van onder- en
bovenwereld en de moord op G. J. Heijn (2008)

Links

http://serbskeinternetnovine.wordpress.com (Serbian Internet News)
http://theserbianarmysrpskaarmija.wordpress.com
http://wacerpolwacerpol.wordpress.com/
http://irisdevries.hi5.com
http://karate-europe.hi5.com
http://srpska.armija.hi5.com
http://slomibo.hi5.com
http://nl.youtube.com/profile_videos?user=LATELIERDELALIBERTE
http://nl.youtube.com/profile_videos?user=VONPIVA
http://nl.youtube.com/profile_videos?user=Slomibo

Slobodan Radojev Mitric

9/11 – The Accusation
Bringing the Guilty to Justice

Willehalm Institute Press Foundation

AMSTERDAM, THE NETHERLANDS

9/11: The Accusation is a translation of the Serbian original *9/11: Tužba* published in 2011 by the author in his *L'Atelier de la Liberté* (Laboratory of Freedom) in Amsterdam.

© English translation: 2011 Robert Jan Kelder

Cover Design: Slobodan Mitric
Translation: Nadin Jovanovic
Redaction and Layout Interior: Robert Jan Kelder
Reading Editor: David Gilmartin
Second Updated and Corrected Printing: June 2011

ISBN/EAN: 978-90-73932-00-5
NUR Code: 339
NUR Description: True Crime

Willehalm Institute Press Foundation
P.O. Box 16621, 1001 RC
Amsterdam, The Netherlands

In the US: Willehalm of Orange Foundation
c/o Robert Morningstar
214 W. 92nd. St. Apt. 3E
NY, NY 10025

info@willehalm.nl
www.willehalmpress.org
http://.911-theaccusation.blogspot.com
http://.willehalminstitute.blogspot.com

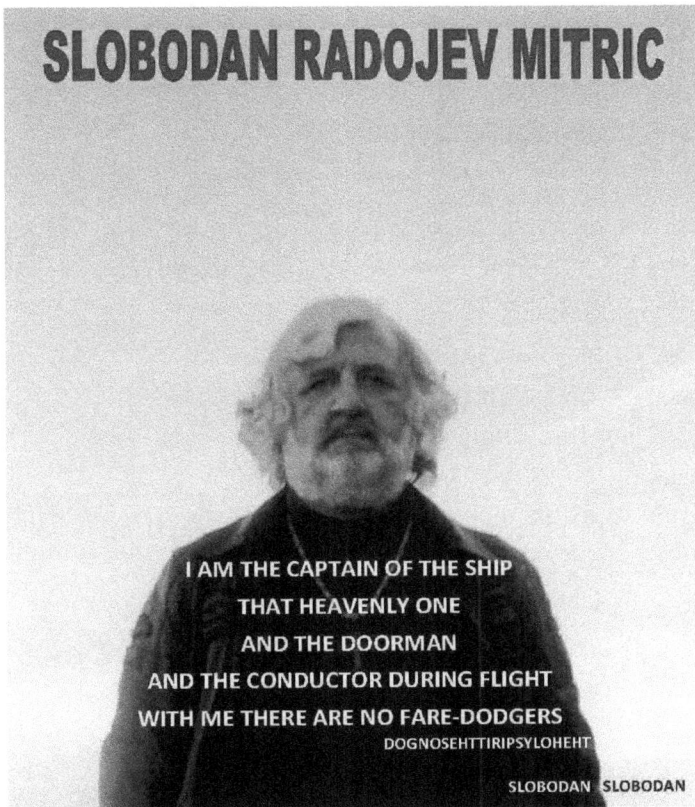

SLOBODAN RADOJEV MITRIC

I AM THE CAPTAIN OF THE SHIP
THAT HEAVENLY ONE
AND THE DOORMAN
AND THE CONDUCTOR DURING FLIGHT
WITH ME THERE ARE NO FARE-DODGERS
DOGNOSEHTTIRIPSYLOHEHT

SLOBODAN SLOBODAN

I dedicate this novel to my deceased beloved wife Iris, to my deceased foster father General Raymond J. Healey, former CIA director for Asia and Europe, and all members of Reserve Police International and of course to all victims of Operation Twins (9/11) from 1982 until 2001.

Slobodan Radojev Mitric

LIST OF CONTENTS

Appendices

Foreword by the Author

This novel is a modern fairytale, for they asked me for the living truth. I asked for one hundred thousand Euros in return to reconstruct the second and third volumes of the novel *Operation Twins* that I had started in 1982 and completed in 1986, when the CIA however confiscated them.

The first volume was excerpted in the early nineties in the magazine *The Serbian Army* and then published in 1999 in the original Serbian under the title *Operacija Blizanci*.

My publisher and his bosses promised in early 2010 that they would give me € 100,000, if I would reconstruct the missing parts 2 and 3.

I began to write, but I received no money; the promise was, as people say - a promise for the joy of fools.

We then agreed in early July 2010 to write a few chapters called "9 /11 - The Accusation" for which they would give me €10.000 so I could pay my rent, electricity and heating while living on dry bread and water until the whole novel would be completed. And when the novel was finished, they would succeed in finding sponsors for the whole novel, and so would pay me the rest of the fee of €100.000.

I wrote the first chapter and was given a down payment of € 1,000.

However, when I confided to my publisher that the leading actors in the novel "9 /11: The Accusation" were Jerries (Germans), suddenly all went downhill.

Every day he invented a new lie. In fact, my publisher and his bosses hoped that they would find the names of the characters they had in mind, names of Jews, in the book "9 /11 – The Accusation."

Because I only write fairytales, I could not agree to that. In fairytales you cannot lie, but imbue imagination with will.

Therefore, I thanked my publisher and told him that he could not publish this novel, but instead only a real publisher, who praises and appreciates true, modern fairy tales.

In the mean time, the difficulties have been ironed out somewhat: the advance edition has been translated and will be presented from May 24 to 26 at BookExpo America 2011 in New York City under the title *9/11- The Accusation/ Bringing the Guilty to Justice.*

Slobodan Radojev Mitric

Foreword by Rade Bozovic

It is not easy to write fairytales in a world dominated by an overly harsh reality and the great and exclusive interests of political and financial oligarchs seeking to achieve their goals at the expense of ordinary people.

And lo and behold, Dr. Slobodan Radojev Mitric has decided on such an unusual way of writing.

True, the narrative genre in which he writes is not that of a fairy tale in the true sense of the word. On the contrary, his narrative portrays the exact truth, although theorists of literature would call it a fairytale.

In Dr. Mitric's fairytales only the names of the characters are fictional and even though this often occurs in a symbolic manner, the attentive reader will easily recognize some of them. Because they are here, among us.

So here is a true crime novel reflecting the harsh reality that can be understood as a paraphrase of a fairytale in a world that is no longer naive and often not ours.

Simple language, deadly conversations and a fluid narrative style allow one to read through the novel effortlessly.

And like in a fairytale, everything related in the novel can without a doubt be accepted as the truth. For Slobodan Mitric obviously not only knows his characters well, but also the underlying context. He simply "scans" them.

In a fairytale, things are often made up; here nothing is made up. So much of it seems unreal and surrealistic that it is impossible for the reader to mistake it for a fairytale, an ugly one perhaps.

A fairytale often has a happy ending in order to please every ear and reader. This novel however has no happy ending, because its theme is the ruthless competition for world dominance.

Slobodan Mitric, who has until now published five novels of a similar content and with a similar literary approach, shows with this work as well as the previous ones, that he is a man to whom the truth is more important than anything else; he is not only a diligent and careful chronicler, but also a keen critic of the events that determine and define today's world. He is a reliable witness of our uncertain times.

The author reminds us to be vigilant. Moreover, in the spirit of the title of his novel, he charges all those who, despite the fact that they posses information about the crime, make up their own version of events, thereby trampling not only on their own conscience.

Reading this novel can frighten us, because many things often remain on the surface of our fast-moving and worrisome lives.

And finally, just as the novel has been written with the intention to communicate a clear message about the world we live in, so the publishing house of the original Serbian edition has a metaphorical, great and inspiring name: *L'Atelier de la Liberté* - Laboratory of Freedom!

There is no freedom without brave words; it is good to be reminded of that and this is what the author does in his novels and his life, Dr. Slobodan Radojev Mitric.

Dr. Prof. Rade Bozovic - Former Dean of the Philological Faculty of the University of Belgrade and presently Professor of Oriental Studies. He is a member of the Serbian Writers Union.

Intro by the Publisher Robert J. Kelder

9/11 – The Accusation – Bringing the Guilty to Justice by Slobodan Mitric can be placed in the tradition of engaged writing as exemplified by the famous Open Letter entitled *J'Accuse…!* by the French novelist Emil Zola addressed to the President of the French Republic in 1898, which ultimately resulted in the release from prison of an innocent French officer of Jewish background, Alfred Dreyfus.

In this case, however, as can be read in his address "To the Readers and People of the World" on the back flap, the author is not only accusing the former President of the French Republic Francois Mitterrand of not having acted on the basis of his many forewarnings to prevent the 9/11 attacks, but also many other former heads of states including US presidents George H.W. Bush, Bill Clinton and George W. Bush as well as their intelligence bosses. Furthermore, he accuses President George Bush Jr. of willfully misinforming the American public and the world about the identity of the real perpetrators by shifting all the blame onto Osama bin Laden, who, even though right after 9/11 had denied all responsibility for this crime, was recently brutally executed as the leader of the responsible party without, as his next of kin have complained in an Open Letter in the New York Times, a fair trial or incriminating evidence.

Granted, these accusations leveled at the high and mighty of this world will appear, for many, at first sight preposterous. But there will also be readers, who do not reject these grave charges outright as ludicrous and instead consider them seriously with an open mind. For them this book may mark a breakthrough in the almost ten year long quest to bear witness to the truth and bring all those really responsible, either directly and indirectly, for the 9/11 attacks to justice, thereby not only revealing that the liquidation of Bin Laden was a miscarriage of justice, but also exonerating the so-called Islamic hijackers from all blame.

This may appear to be too apodictic a statement, but that the author's allegations do indeed deserve a fair hearing is not only due to the strength of his novel itself with its many new, even startling and sensational insights and detailed descriptions. It is also justified by the undeniable fact that the author had issued many forewarning of 9/11, based on his inside knowledge from his teamwork as a counter-intelligence operative, who had managed to infiltrate the nerve center of the perpetrators centered around a mysterious figure called "The Hague Mouse" and a covert terrorist group of neo-Nazi's, radical anarchists and Islamists called "Titans".

These forewarnings appeared first in the form of his trilogy *Operation Twins* published in Amsterdam in 1982, which earned him an honorary degree in law from a Police College in Tucson, Arizona, in 1986. This atomic counter-espionage novel describes the run-up to a nuclear confrontation between America and the Soviet Union at the very end of the second millennium, which after it had been avoided by grounding all airplanes (Y2K), was then postponed to September 11, 2001. That 9/11, as Ch. 10 "This is only a conventional rocket. Do you want war? Just tell me!" shows, was indeed an abortive attempt to start World War III is something which, to my knowledge, only US author Webster Tarpley has so far alluded to. In Ch. 6 the double-dealing role in this nuclear confrontation on the part of an "Australian" computer programmer, who in the nineties had bought a house in the central canal district of Amsterdam, is revealed. The records show that at this address mentioned, Herengracht 106, lived the founder of the software company MicroMuse, Chris Dawes, who died instantly in a "car crash" in 1999 in England.

The second form of these forewarnings consisted of photos of large planes nose diving onto vital targets in the US and Europe with explosives being detonated in these buildings from nearby locations. These photo's were published in the author's magazine *The Serbian Army* in the early nineties with accompanying letters sent to the appropriate US intelligence and political authorities and heads of state of their allies in the East and West, i.e. almost a decade in advance of the catastrophic events of that fateful day. And not only forewarnings of 9/11. For as his letter as World Atomic Counter-espionage (WACE) director to the CIA, dated December 20, 1988 in Chapter 3 "Aircraft Fall From The Sky like Raindrops" shows, he also attempted to prevent the Lockerbie disaster, a forewarning flatly rejected by the recipient on the grounds that this was none of his (Mitric's) business!

As can be read in Ch. 7 "I am that terrorist!" those images of nose diving planes were also shown during the first secret joint American-Russian antiterrorist conference, in which a man named Nick steps forward to reveal that he is that "terrorist" appearing in the foreground of these photos. This figure is Nikola Kavaya, a former bodyguard of President Kennedy, and adjunct-director of WACE and as such a close associate of its director Slobodan Mitric: "We caught sharks with human bait [i.e. Kavavya], not with a firefly. This was seven years before the attacks. Now everyone has their own theory. Judge for yourself!" (Recently Mitric posted on one of his Serbian blogs *Juzni Sloveni* a long, revealing interview with this legendary figure in Serbia, who, after he had been contracted from the US a few years ago to write his memoirs, died from food poisoning in a Belgrade restaurant under suspicious circumstances.)

However, the CIA confiscated the second and third volumes of *Operation Twins* in 1986, thereby abruptly ending efforts by the author to bring his book to the screen with the backing of then President Reagan. Fortunately, a copy of volume one was salvaged, which was then published by the author in Serbian his L'Atelier de la Liberté in Amsterdam in 1999 and by the Willehalm Institute Press in English in 2005, followed by an excerpt of the second volume of this trilogy in 2006.

Some of the 9/11 forewarning images from the first volume of *Operation Twins* that were published in *The Serbian Army* in the nineties have been included here in the annotated appendices, not as water-tight proof that this is indeed a true crime novel (some names and places have been changed), but as irrefutable evidence that the author knows from his own experience and observation (sometimes from secret films of the described scenes) what he is talking about and should therefore be taken dead seriously.

The 25 appendices include other illustrated articles from *The Serbian Army*, letters and statements by the author, title and back pages from his previous true crime novels such as *The Golden Tip* with a number of references to this book, and pre-announcements of two new books, one being on the real background to the murder of

Theo van Gogh and a science fiction novel about the imminent invasion of 12 space ships entitled *God's Secrets*. It is to this publication that the inscription "I am the captain of the ship" on the author's photo page refers.

Of special interest may be his documented CV, which gives an insight not only into his professional life, but also into the difficult financial, legal, medical and security circumstances under which he has been forced to subsist in The Netherlands for more than three decades. It includes an impressive list of references and feats of arms that may serve to further substantiate the claim that this novel, unbelievable as it may seem at first sight, must be taken as deadly serious.

To what the author has written in his foreword about the difficulties with his publisher in order to get this advanced edition of a larger work to see the light of day, I would now respond with: let bygones be bygones. To objections as those that were made by a member of U.S. 9/11 internet forum to the publisher to the effect that his efforts to raise through international "crowd funding" the necessary money for the writing and publication of this novel amount to an immoral, commercial exploitation of the victims of 9/11, I can only reply that anyone only slightly aware under what conditions this work came into being, would not dream of making such a remark.

With this new book the author is again sticking out his neck, this time in a valiant effort to bring to justice those responsible for allowing 9/11 to happen. As such, it may already contain sufficient material for a judicial court, be it an American one or one attached to the United Nations, to start a preliminary inquest, for which extra material in the form of the whole trilogy *Operation Twins*, under the conditions mentioned by the author in his foreword and in the contract on p. 160 – which he needs in order to survive and to finally secure pro-active legal and medical aid and attention – can then be made available.

I sincerely hope that these conditions can be met, for as I wrote to the Englishman Graham R ,who kindly donated money to help get this project further off the ground: "This book can then truly make world history by solving one of the greatest mysteries, if not

the greatest, of this young millennium and thereby at last bring the
true perpetrators of 911 to justice."

Acknowledgements

For invaluable assistance in making the writing and publication of
this book possible, I extend my sincere thanks to the following persons: first of course to the author for having the iron will to complete this work under almost unbearable circumstances, which
would have long ago broken any normal human being, then to Prof.
Rade Bozovic, from the University of Belgrade for writing a foreword, to Nadin Jovanovic for her part in the translation from the
Serbian to English, to my old friend David Gilmartin for his excellent editing of the text on short notice, to Debbie Rooijakkers for her
InDesign work on the cover, to the printers ScanLaser in Zaandam,
Holland for quick and reliable service, to Iwanjka Geerdink, quixot-
ic founder of NovaGlobe, who, at an impasse during which it
seemed that the still required advance to finish writing the novel
would never be gotten and a Karate Bob Benefit Fund started on
FaceBook brought no solace either, suddenly appeared on the scene
and with his splendid intuitive investment infused new life into this
project. He also kindly agreed to accompany me to New York City
to present this book at the Writer's Booth #5048 at BookExpo
America in the Jacob Javitts Convention Center from May 24 to 26.
Finally, I thank my brother Johannes, who, although already having
seen his previous investments in the Willehalm Foundation yield
practically nothing in return, did lend me now and then enough to
just make the grade.

Update for the Second Printing

This second printing for the US market is being prepared in New York City
after having presented the first advance edition at BookExpo America on
May 25 to, among others, filmmaker Michael Moore of "Fahrenheit 9/11"
fame, who has not (yet) given any reaction. On June 2, I appeared on the
Kevin Smith Show aired from Arizona for an almost two hour long interview on this book, its author and the author's foster father General Healey,
who appeared to the show's researches to have left no traces on the internet.
However, a day after the show I received the following letter from Kevin
Smith: "You might be interested in knowing that I have finally found a
reference to MAJ. General Raymond J. Healey. Here is the quote from an

article by Devvy Kidd: 'There are a lot of people in this country who have been aware of the possibility that there were survivors from that incident. One of the people I have had dialogue with over the years regarding KAL 007 just passed away Nov. 3, 1999. Major General Raymond Healey was a wonderful, wonderful, dedicated American and our country has lost one of its great freedom fighters. General Healey and a number of other concerned citizens had been in contact with some other groups who had done some quiet investigative work through international channels and swear Americans from that flight have been seen alive in Russia in camps. General Healey was just as enraged as I have been about KAL 007 - another big fat lie shoved down the throats of the American people. (...) The link is here: http://www.devvy.com/kal007_19991120.html'

At the beginning of that day's show (June 3) Kevin Smith went at great length to report on the 'rediscovery' of this great, but almost forgotten American freedom fighter.

Having meanwhile become a member of the We Are Change NYC group, I positioned myself on June 4 at the usual Ground Zero meeting place, rolled up a banner with two images from the book and handed out some leaflets. With WAC member Victor Cintron, we shot a 16 min. film, which appeared on June 10 on YouTube. On June 11, the newly formed WAC NYC Group entitled "9/11 – The Accusation" with its members called The Accusers will have its first meet-up at this Ground Zero venue. (Links to all the above information and more can be found on http://911-TheAccusation.blogspot.com).

On closing this update, I want to thank my new friend and colleague Robert J. Morningstar for the hospitality and good cheer he extended to Iwanjka Geerdink and myself on our visit to New York where, Lady Luck willing, I plan to return to launch the complete edition of this book on 9/11.

PROLOGUE

PARACHUTISTS

THE FIRST TEAM

Schmidt opens the hatch of the aircraft. At a height of 33,000 feet he jumps head first into the abyss, followed by Rita and Dolf. They plummet down like arrows. All three breathe oxygen from special tanks. Far below them lies a dense cloud cover. In dozens of seconds, the trio is lost in water vapor. Immediately afterwards they see vast plains.

At a height of less than 1000 feet Schmidt pulls the handle. The parachute opens. His friends follow him. Soon all three successfully hit the dry grass.

All untie the parachutes, pack them and take off their back-packs and their parachute overalls, which they had put over their street clothes.

Schmidt produces a small military shovel and quickly digs a hole. Rita and Dolf do the same. Within minutes, they bury their parachutes and equipment.

Schmidt draws a cell phone from his leather pilot jacket and taps a number. Immediately he gets connected. Although they are far from any inhabited area, he whispers, "Hello! Black eagle here"

"Are you all right!"

"Yes! All three of us are alive and well."

"Nobody saw you!"

"Nobody!"

"Okay! Good luck."

"Thanks!"

The three of them walk towards a highway.

*

The modified Boeing 767-200, American Airlines Flight 1, flies toward New York.

A transmitter sends out signals.

The computer in the plane responds by decreasing its altitude. Underneath the aircraft appear tall buildings. The computer further reduces its altitude to 1000 feet.

The roar of the low-flying plane causes New Yorkers to look up.

A taxi driver peers through his side window. Waving a clenched fist, he yells out, "The route of the pilot is not normal. The building will get hit!"

His customer looks at the sky. "Maybe the pilot's drunk."

At exactly 46 minutes after 8 o'clock, the nose of the Boeing 767-200, in which 200 kg. of high-grade uranium was hidden, hits the North Tower of the World Trade Center at full speed, exactly at the office where the transmitter was located. Immediately there is a strong explosion and then the fuel tank explodes in turn, causing a huge fire that spreads at lightning speed. All government employees on that floor are instantly burned alive.

Panic arises throughout the tower. People run toward the elevators and through emergency exits into the stairwells. They push and shove each other. Women are screaming hysterically and falling down on the marble floors. Men are trampling them. Everyone seeks to vacate the building as quickly as possible.

New Yorkers on the street look up in stunned silence at the huge fireball. Black smoke rising into the air seems to have returned from the days when the natives of the newly discovered continent sent smoke signals.

The taxi driver hits both hands on the steering wheel. "What did I tell you!"

His customer nods! "Yes! Yes! Unfortunately, you were right!"

THE FOURTH TEAM

Helga opens the hatch of the aircraft. At a height of 33,000 feet she jumps head first into the abyss, followed by Karl and Robert. They plummet down like arrows. All three breathe oxygen from special tanks. Far below them lies a dense cloud cover. In dozens of seconds, the trio is lost in water vapor. Immediately afterwards they see vast plains.

At a height of less than 1000 feet, Helga pulls the handle. The parachute opens. Her friends follow her. Soon all three safely hit the dry grass.

All untie the parachutes and pack them neatly. They take off their backpacks and parachute overalls, which they had put over their street clothes.

Helga produces a small military shovel and quickly digs a hole. Robert and Karl do the same. Within minutes, they bury the parachutes and their equipment.

Helga takes a cell phone from her leather pilot jacket and taps a number. Immediately she gets connected. "Hello!" she whispers. "Black eagle number 4 here."

"Are you all right!"

"Yes!"

"No one saw you!"

"No! What about the other birds?"

"One has successfully found the nest."

"Excellent! What now?"

"Act according to instructions."

"Okay! Bye!"

"Good luck."

THE THIRD TEAM

"Hello! Black eagle number 3 here."

"Are you all right!"

"Yes!"

"No one saw you!"

"No! What about the other birds."

"First Eagle scored a hit!"

"Bravo Gill!"

From the speaker of the phone sounds a hoarse voice. "Bitch! Don't mention my name!"

"Sorry! I'm excited."

21

"We'll talk about that later. The fourth eagle died in flight."
"How come?"
"We don't know. Follow instructions."
"Will do! Don't worry!"
"Good luck!"
The threesome walk toward a highway.

*

The modified Boeing 757, United Airlines Flight 93, flies on toward Washington. Suddenly the plane is hit by a rocket. The plane plummets. Within seconds the nose of the plane, in which 200 kg. of high-grade uranium was hidden, hits the ground. Big explosions are echoed. The plane explodes into a hundred pieces. Two F-15 fighter jets fly over the downed aircraft.

From the speaker of the first jet sounds a happy voice. "Good shot Lisa."

"Thanks Bill!"

THE SECOND TEAM

The modified Boeing 767, United Airlines Flight 175, is heading for New York.

The transmitter sends out signals.

The computer in the Boeing reduces its altitude. Underneath the aircraft appear skyscrapers. The computer further reduces the altitude to 1000 feet.

New Yorkers on the street look up and shout in chorus, "Oh my God! Not again!"

At exactly 3 minutes after 9 'o clock, the nose of the Boeing, in which 200 kg. high-grade uranium was hidden, slams at full speed into the South Tower of the World Trade Center, exactly at the office where the transmitter was located. A huge explosion follows. Immediately, the fuel tank explodes, causing a huge fireball that spreads at lightning speed. All employees on that floor are also instantly burnt alive.

New Yorkers are looking up in stunned silence at the infer-

22

no. Black smoke from both towers rises into the air.

The taxi driver and his customer step out of the cab. "Wow, this is no coincidence, I tell you! This is a terrorist attack."

"Yes! Yes!" his customer nods. "You're damn right!"

Chapter 1

SLEEPER

Paris, October 6, 1977

Platform one of the biggest Parisian, and certainly also the biggest European, railway station, is as usual before the departure of trains crowded with people; crowded not only with the passengers, but also with those who came along to say goodbyes to their loved ones and with the many bellboys carrying luggage.

The sound of the whistle drowns out the noise. The conductor closes the door of the last car. The station master waves his flag and with all his breath blows the whistle: "FIIIIIIIII-JUUUUUUUUUUUUUU!"

At exactly 8 P.M. the Paris-Milan express slowly leaves the Northern Station, Gare du Nord. Passengers are waving through open windows while friends run alongside the train waving back a last farewell.

Avdo and Brigit have booked a luxurious first class cabin in the middle of the last sleeping car. As coincidence would have it – if there is such a thing as coincidence in the life of spies and criminals – the Russian trade attaché, General Yuri Smolinski with his young secretary Olga, and the American military attaché, Colonel Arthur Hartman, who is traveling alone, have also booked a cabin in the same car.

Avdo stretches and yawns. "Are you hungry?"

"Yes and no," answers the longhaired beautiful blonde.

"Let's go to the restaurant then."

"You think that's wise?"

"Pfff! Why not?!"

"Perhaps we'll draw suspicion."

Avdo reaches for the door handle and nods his head toward the

24

entrance so as to follow him. "Nonsense! We'll draw more suspicion, if we stay in our cabin all the time. Don't worry; it's not the first time that I've worked in this sort train."

Brigit hesitates. "All the more reason to be cautious."

Avdo opens the door. "Ah! Follow me or would you rather stay here and get laid?"

The Parisienne quickly gets up and follows him.

The restaurant is not crowded; here and there a few guests are enjoying a delicious meal. At a table next to the bar sits the Russian trade attaché and his unusually short-haired blond secretary.

Avdo notices that the Russian is holding a diplomatic briefcase on his lap.

A young waitress shows Avdo and Brigit to a table. After the new guests sit down, she hands them a menu. "What would you like to order?"

"One of your finest bottles of French wine please. We'll order the food later," Avdo says.

Brigit frowns. "For me only mineral water please."

Avdo teases her. "Wet or dry?"

"Sparkling."

The waitress nods. "Okay, a liter of wine and a bottle of mineral water." She goes to the bar.

"You think it's wise to drink on the job?" Brigit asks angrily.

Avdo smiles and waves it aside. "Don't worry dear."

"Don't worry, don't worry! You promised you wouldn't drink."

"I promised that I wouldn't touch you, but the night is still young."

A crimson blush spreads on Brigit's cheeks."Are you joking?"

"Just wait until I lift those long legs of yours. Or would you rather have that circumcised sultan of mine from behind?"

Brigit clenches her fist. "If you dare touch me, I will break your nose!"

"Before or after?"

Brigit blushes again. "You're disgusting."

"Bet that you'll love me?"

"Pfff! Avdo please, we agreed no pleasure during work. Besides, you're not my type and you know very well that I'm a married woman."

"Okay, okay woman, I'm just joking."

At about ten o'clock the restaurant begins to empty. Avdo wipes his mustache with his napkin, strokes his goatee and gets up from the table. He walks over to the bar and takes out his wallet. "How much do I owe you?"

The waitress fetches the bill and reads aloud, "Two liters of wine, 70 francs. Two bottles of mineral water, 10 francs. Two portions of chateaubriand, 140 francs. Two servings of ice cream, 20 francs and two espressos, 10 francs."

Avdo quickly offers her three large bills. "That makes a total of three hundred francs."

The waitress smiles. "You're wrong sir; it's two hundred and fifty!"

"Three hundred gorgeous. Three hundred, the remainder is for you."

The waitress utters a shriek of joy. "Thank you very much sir!"

With one hand on his sunglasses Avdo leans toward the waitress and whispers, "This is just an advance."

The waitress spreads her hands. "I don't understand"

Avdo pets her on the shoulder and winks. "For our love next time when I'm alone."

The waitress blushes. "Are you joking?"

"Who knows? Who knows? For such a beautiful diva I would give all my millions that I have yet to earn."

Laughing, he returns to his table. Brigit gets up."Please buy me a bottle of mineral water to go."

Avdo walks back to the bar and notices the Russian leaving the restaurant.

The waitress looks at him. Avdo winks at her. "My woman is thirsty like a fish for water. Please give me a bottle of mineral water."

The waitress quickly takes out a bottle from the fridge, while Avdo takes out his wallet. "How much do I owe you?"

"It's a gift to your lady."

Avdo takes the bottle. "Thank you very much. Don't forget our deal."

"Are you joking?"

"You'll see I'm not kidding."

"Goodnight sir"

"See ye."

Avdo returns to Brigit. Both leave the restaurant. The waitress waves to them. Avdo returns to their compartment by himself, while Brigit goes to the end of the car and enters the conductor's compartment. "Good evening sir"

"Good evening, good evening!"

Brigit winks and hands him her and Avdo's fake passports. "Please do not wake us if it's not necessary. He's my lover."

The bald conductor quickly gets up and takes the documents. He opens her passport and smiles friendly. "Are you a baroness?"

"Something like that."

"Don't worry madam. Custom officials and police rarely check in the first class sleepers. I'll personally see to it that they don't disturb you."

"Thank you very much! Good night sir."

"Good night, madam Baroness."

Brigit leaves the compartment, swinging her hips on the way to her own compartment. She is more than sure that the conductor is watching her every move.

Avdo takes off his glasses, puts them in their case and opens the zipper of a sport bag. He inserts the sunglasses case in the bag and pulls out a doctor's stethoscope. Putting the ear-tubes to his ears, he presses the diaphragm to the wall and listens carefully.

From the compartment of the U.S. military attaché he hears snoring. *Hrrooooo! Hrrrr! Hrrrrrrrr!*

"The Ami is asleep," Avdo whispers. He turns around to the other side of compartment, gently pushes Brigit aside and kneels next to her. He presses the diaphragm to the adjacent wall of the cabin and listening, he hears groans, *Aaah! Aaa! Aaah! Ooo! Ooo! Yes, Yuri! Daa! Aaaa! Aaaa!*

27

"Did they fall asleep?" Brigit whispers.

Avdo takes off the stethoscope and hands it to her. "No idea, I can't hear anything. You listen," he bluffs.

"Well, then they're sleeping".

He gently strokes her hair."You listen a moment, woman."

Brigit puts the stethoscope on and kneels down on the seat, presses the diaphragm on the wall and listens. *Ooh. Yuri! Ooh! Yes! Yeah! Ooooh!*

Avdo smacks her on the buttocks. "Are they still screwing?"

Brigit takes off the stethoscope and throws it at him. She gets up, stretches her knees and sits down. "You really are impossible! Shame on you!"

Avdo gets up and with both hands grabs Brigit by her long blond hair."What do you think?" he whispers. "They'll take a long time. It would be a shame for me to lose time."

Brigit blushes "Avdo please don't!" she says loudly.

With one hand he opens his fly and with the other pulls her head toward him.

"Ssssht you will wake the American."

"You're crazy."

"Yes I am! Sssht."

Brigit ceases to protest.

The train stops. Avdo puts his dick back into place and closes his fly. Brigit wipes her mouth with a handkerchief and runs a hand through her hair.

Avdo looks at his gold Omega and gets up. "It's midnight. Looks like we're at the border. I'm going to check."

"I have to go to the bathroom."

"Are you crazy? It's forbidden to go to the bathroom when the train is standing still."

"I have to go."

Avdo grabs her between her legs: "Be patient a while. Close your little treasury with your hand!"

She pushes him away. "Bastard!"

"Ha ha ha!" he chuckles. "But you sucked this bastard well."

"Bastard! If you tell anyone I'll kill you!"

"Ha ha ha!"

"Just keep laughing. You think I'm joking?"

"Don't worry, woman".

Both of them step out into the hallway. Brigit goes to the ladies room. Avdo opens a window and pokes his head out. He notices a few custom officials and police officers entering the second class cars and notes that he was right about being at the border.

In the meantime Brigit returns. "What kind of train is this?" she says angrily. "They don't even have toilet paper."

"I'll clean it properly for you when we're in Switzerland."

Brigit grabs the door hook. "Asshole!"

"Keep swearing."

Both enter the cabin. Avdo locks the door. After a while they hear footsteps in the hall. Brigit takes a sip from her bottle of mineral water and chokes. *Ugh! Ugh! Ugh!*

Avdo puts his finger on his lips. *Psst!*

Brigit calms down. The footsteps pass by. Shortly afterwards the train starts moving. Ten minutes later, it stops again. "Switzerland!" Brigit whispers.

"Don't worry. The Swiss never check the people travelling in the sleeping cars."

"Oh!"

"Yeah! It's an unwritten law. They know that people travelling in sleepers bring dirty money and fill the Swiss banks."

After a few minutes the trains starts moving. With his stethoscope Avdo checks the noise in the compartment of the Russian diplomat. A smile appears on his face. "Both are snoring. If you don't believe me, check it for yourself."

Brigit throws a dark glance at him. "No thanks! I believe you."

"Come on, check it."

"Fuck off."

Avdo grins and goes to the other side of the cabin to check the situation in the cabin of the American military attaché. He comes back quickly. "The Ami snores and snores." He removes the stethoscope from his ears and gives it to Brigit. "Hold this!"

"What am I supposed to do?"

"Take it, woman! You listen, while I work."

Brigit hesitates a moment. "You're not going to fool me again, are you?"

Avdo takes a small hand drill from his bag. "Don't worry. Come on, let's go to work."

Brigit connects to stethoscope to her ears and looks at her partner with suspicion. Avdo places the drill bit against the wall of the Russian diplomat's cabin. "Go on, listen!"

Brigit presses the microphone against the wall and listens. "It's okay, they're snoring."

"Now you see that I didn't pull your leg this time," he whispers as he begins to turn the handle of the silent hand drill.

"This is the only time that you didn't lie."

With a grin on his face he goes on drilling. The 30 cm long diamond bit cuts its way through the wall as if it were butter. Brigit is listening and nods that all is well. In less than a minute, Avdo feels that the bit has forced its way into the cabin of the Russian diplomat. He skillfully removes the drill and from his bag takes a small can with the label: shaving cream. Then he fastens a plastic tube to the small opening of the can of shaving cream. The other end of the tube he presses into the hole that he just drilled in the wall of the Russian diplomat's cabin. He presses the button and hears the quiet hissing of the first class Czech-made sleeping gas. Brigit is still listening. Avdo looks on his watch and after a few minutes removes the tube from the hole in the wall. "I gave them a double dose," he grins."They'll wake up in two days."

"Are you crazy! What if they die?"

"Don't worry woman, I'm not a child."

"I hope to God you're right."

Avdo nods to his partner to move to the other side. There he repeats everything in the direction of the cabin of the American military attaché. When finished he puts all the tools back in his bag.

"And now what?" Brigit whispers.

"Stop whispering, you dumb blonde," he answers loudly. "Now I could screw you as long as you want, if I had some time, and even if you scream like a merry, they cannot hear us anymore."

Brigit's face assumes the color of a ripe tomato. "Who's the dumbbell here?"

Avdo takes a big pincer from his bag and gives it to his partner. He puts surgical gloves and a gasmask on. He grabs the door handle and grumbles, "I'm joking, woman. Let's get to work."

Brigit relaxes. They go out into the hallway. Avdo inserts a special key that only conductors possess into the door lock of the Russian diplomat. He opens the lock and slowly opens the door a little. At once he notes that the Russian has fastened a metal safety chain on the door. He motions his partner to give him the pincer. Skillfully he positions the chain into the head of the pincer and squeezes forcefully. The chain breaks like a sprig. Avdo gives the pincer to Brigit. "Go back to our cabin and wait for the signal," he mutters.

"Okay." She returns to the cabin.

Avdo then steps into the cabin of the Russian diplomat, locks the door behind him and turns on the light. General Yuri Smolinksi and his stunningly beautiful secretary Olga are lying in bed naked as Adam and Eve in Paradise.

Avdo searches through the Russian diplomat's uniform hanging on the wall. Quickly he slides the wallet of the man into his own pocket and then empties a handbag of the blond Olga. He places his hand under Yuri Smolinksi's pillow and touches a piece of cold iron. A soft smile lights up his face.

Skillfully he stores the Russian pistol under his belt. He picks up the diplomatic attaché case and knocks twice on the wall, then twice again and waits a moment. It is answered with knocks on the door, twice and then twice again. He turns the light out and leaves the cabin. Quickly he removes the gasmask and locks the door. Together they return to their cabin.

"A good haul!" Avdo boasts as he places the diplomatic attaché case on the bed. The locks he opens with a special key. He opens his eyes wide-open: The case is packed with stacks of $100 bills.

"Wow," Brigit exclaims from happiness.

"What did I tell you? There is at least half a million." Avdo quickly closes the case and looks at his watch. "Let's hurry! In an hour we'll be in Lausanne."

Brigit spreads her arms in contentment. "But we've got enough money now!"

"Are you crazy? We continue."

Avdo motions with his hand to the window. "Close the curtains!" As Brigit walks to the window he quickly hides the Russian pistol in his bag, takes out the pincer and says, "Follow me!"

They go out into the hallway. Avdo puts on his gasmask and skillfully unbolts the door to the cabin of the American diplomat. Slowly he pushes the door open; light hits their faces. A soft smile appears on his face. "I don't need the pincer, "he mumbles. "This idiot forgot to put on the safety chain. Go on back and wait till I gave you the signal again."

Brigit returns to their cabin. Avdo quickly enters the cabin of the American diplomat and locks the door.

Colonel Arthur Hartman lies in bed in uniform.

Avdo notices an almost empty bottle of Scotch whisky on the floor. "Cowboy, you didn't need the gas," he grumbles to himself. Quickly he goes through the pockets of the American diplomat. He puts the diplomat's wallet in his pocket and places his hand under the pillow, groping. There he finds nothing. Again he searches through Colonel Hartman's pockets. Nothing. With some effort, he turns him over on his stomach. Nothing again. "Cowboy, where is your gun," Avdo grumbles to himself." He inspects the cabin and sees hanging on the wall a military overcoat. Quickly he removes the coat from the hanger. Under the coat is a belt with a holster. Avdo removes the weapon, a 44 Magnum that flashes strongly. "Hey Ami, Ami!" he jokes to himself. "Thank you for all eternity."

Avdo sticks the revolver under his belt and looks on the floor. Only then he notices a diplomatic suitcase. He lifts it up and feels that it is quite heavy. He knocks twice on the wall in the direction of his cabin, after that twice more. The answer comes fast: two knocks on the door and then twice again.

Avdo turns out the light and grumbles to the sleeping American, "Drunkard. You'll have to sleep in the dark." He enters the hallway, places the suitcase on the floor and takes of his mask. Quickly he locks the cabin and bends down to pick up the suitcase.

Together they return to their cabin. Avdo places the suitcase on the bed, walks to the door to bolt it and removes his gloves. "Let me drink some of your water!"

Brigit gives him the bottle. Avdo takes a few sips, gives the bottle back and says, "Thanks a lot.
Let us see now what our dear Ami has given us."

With a master key Avdo unbolts the lock and opens the lid. Strong flashes almost blind their eyes.

"Diamonds! Gold!" Both exclaim in unison.

Avdo grabs a hand full of diamonds and pours them into the open hands of his partner. "Now you are really a baroness!"

Brigit puts the diamonds back in the box. "Oh, Avdo! We're rich!"

"So, what did I tell you!" He lifts up a gold bar, looks at the hallmark and gives the bar to his partner. "Have a look at this, girl!"

"Dear God, where does Ami get a suitcase full of Hitler's gold."

"And diamonds!"

"Well, maybe his father was a Nazi and robbed my Jewish family."

"Asshole, what a thief! But he ran into a super thief!"

Avdo opens a half empty, big suitcase and puts both diplomatic attaché cases inside. Then he looks at his watch. "We still have half an hour before we reach Lausanne. Come on, let's see what your talents are. Go and lure that old prick into he toilet. Tell him there's no more toilet paper. At least that's no lie. Suck him a few minutes if necessary. I already taught you that trick. Don't let him get out of the toilet, until I steal our passports again."

Brigit blushes. "But that too we didn't agree on."

"Now we have. Come on, hurry up."

"You're not going to tell that to David, are you?"

"Are you crazy? From now on you're my mistress."

Brigit's face turns red again. As she leaves the cabin, Avdo hits her gently with an open hand on her bottom. "Don't disappoint me, girl!"

"Asshole!"

The Express train stops in Lausanne. Avdo and Brigit leave the sleeping car in a hurry. A dark man, very small as far as his height is concerned, approaches them. Standing on the tips of his shoes, he kisses Brigit on her cheeks. "Hello darling, is everything okay?"

"Yes! Yes!" she says, bending down to answer his kisses.

All three disappear quickly to the exit, while the conductor of the sleeper, peeking through the window, muuters, "Dear God, what a beautiful whore!"

*

The trio steps into a limousine parked near the main entrance of the station. David starts the engine and turns on the lights. Avdo quickly removes his glasses, fake beard and moustache. Brigit does the same with her blond wig and long fake eye-lashes that she gives to Avdo, who puts everything in a plastic back together with the fake passports. Then she combs her long auburn hair and applies lipstick on her thick lips.

David presents Avdo with a new passport. "Here you go, Mister Antonio Toro. Now you're Italian," he jokes.

Avdo opens the passport. "Antonio Toro? Nice first name and nice surname, easy to remember. Well, if I wasn't circumcised, I could also right away change my faith."

David just smiles. "Come and join us, that at least presents no problem."

"Ha, ha! Babo would kill me.".

"The day, month and year of your birth I left as it was in your original passport."

"Thanks. That means I was born in Turin?"

"Yes!"

The Citroën moves. As they leave the center of Lausanne and take the freeway in the direction of Geneva, Brigit is already half asleep.

"She's tired," Avdo says.

"Women are women," David grins.

"Where are we going?"

"To my villa on the shore of Lake Geneva."

"The Lake of Geneva is big."

"It's located exactly between Geneva and Bellerive."

"Oh!" Avdo says as if he really knows where that is.

"You know where it is?"

"Near the Lake of Geneva."

David starts to laugh. "Ha ha ha! You've always got a ready-made answer."

"That's my profession, isn't it?"

David suppresses his laughter. "The richest people in the world live there, all of them Arabs. I'm the only Jew there."

"Even one is too much," Avdo says to tease him. "I swear by Allah."

David laughs again. "That's a good one. But don't forget that your people are descended from us."

"How's that?"

"According to Ismael, Avdo!"

"Ooh!"

"Ooh, ooh, you only say ooh. You have no idea who Ismael was."

Avdo admits it. "The communists have forbidden our belief in Allah."

"I know it, Avdo. I know. With these precious stones it will be easy for me to get rid of them."

Avdo rubs with his thumb on his light fingered forefinger. "Hopefully you'll get a good price."

"The best. They pay the full market value. "

"Fiiiiiiiiiii!"

"That's why I'm telling you. I live in one of the world's best diamond markets."

Avdo scratches the back of his neck. "Now I understand how you got that house at Avenue FOC in Paris."

"You forget the castle in England."

"Oooh! Yeah!"

"Ha ha ha! You with your ooh's. You had no idea that I also own that costly real estate. Yet I admire you. You're a master of your trade."

"To each his trade, David."

"So it is, Avdo. And together we'll be stronger. Only, keep your fingers away from Brigit, please. Otherwise there will be war."

Avdo looks David deep in the eyes. "Eh, David, David. I swear to you by Allah. I won't even think of such a thing. Man, Brigit I respect as my sister."

"Agreed, Avdo."

"Word of honor."

The limousine stops in front of a big iron gate on the Chemin de Sousa Kan Street. David presses on the remote control. The gate opens and the Citroën drives into a large courtyard. Avdo and David get out of the car in front of an enormous villa. The building is lit up with big reflectors.

Avdo fancies himself to be in a castle from the Arabian Tales of Thousand and One Nights. "David, man. You don't mean to say that this is all yours!"

"Everything, Avdo, everything. The estate even goes as far as the shore of Lake Geneva. But, dear Avdo, I've run up a big debt."

"Eh, David, may God help me run such debts once."

"Don't worry, Avdo. Just hold on to me."

"I will, David, I will."

David opens the door of the Citroën and shakes his beautiful, young wife. "Wake up, darling! We're home already."

Sleepy, Brigit has difficulties getting out of the car. She embraces David, who staggers. Avdo quickly steps in to embrace both of them to prevent them from falling. All three hurry inside to a luxurious salon on the main floor.

*

La Santé Prison, Paris. October 10, 1987

Avdo lies in bed in his cell. He could not sleep the whole night from joy, and that is not surprising, today after all he will be released. He stops staring at the ceiling and ends his recollections of the period that he was free for the last time in Paris before he ended up in this famous, infamous Parisian prison.

This is his last night after having spent a full ten years in French prisons. Last week he was transferred for the second time to the house of detention of La Santé where he had begun his career as a French prisoner. Before that, Avdo also had a criminal record in the country of his birth. He was even incarcerated in the former Yugoslav political prison Goli Otok.

This time the French police will extradite him from La Santé prison to the town where he was born, Sarajevo. Avdo did not protest against his extradition. He knows that for a couple of thousand dollars he would easily be able to buy a new passport in Sarajevo and that within a week he would be in the West again.

However, this time certainly not in Paris. His destiny had brought him here in La Santé Prison into contact with a rich Dutchman, the head of all radical Dutch anarchists in The Hague, who was jailed only ten days for the embezzlement of some hundred million Dutch guilders and who with the aid of a battery of French and Dutch lawyers arranged to be immediately released in return for a suitcase of money.

The Hague Mouse was fascinated by the methods which landed Avdo in jail and did not want to squeal on his partners. Even when the French police had offered him to be immediately released, if he would give away whom he worked for. But Avdo kept his mouth shut. For several reasons. He did not want to tell anybody, not even the Hague Mouse, why he remained silent.

The Hague Mouse gave him his address and told him that as a result of the Mouse's influence and power he, Avdo, would become as rich as he himself if not even richer and that the door of his luxurious villa in the center of The Hague would always be wide open for him.

Chapter 2

MODERN GLADIATORS

The streets of Karlsruhe, West-Germany, this morning are quiet as usual. In a black limousine, sitting next to the driver are two heavily armed guards of the security service responsible for protecting the Federal Attorney General of West Germany. The limo turns left off Hans Thomas Street and slowly drives into Waldstrasse.

Thirty feet ahead, the driver is forced to step on his brake. With much luck, the limousine scrapes just 10 inches of the bumper of a dirty minivan ripe for demolition, located in the middle of the street. On the right side of the van stands a grey-haired old woman.

The driver presses his horn. *Tuuu! Tuuu! Tuuu!*

Loudly cursing, the granny lifts her hands to heaven. "Shitty engine!"

The public prosecutor folds his morning newspaper *Die Welt* , "Ask her," he resolutely orders, "to put that wreck on the side of the road!"

One of the bodyguards presses a button to open his window and says with a stern voice, "Are you mad? Put that wreck on the side of the road!"

The old woman nods her head up and down and waves her hands. "The engine is broken, sir."

The second bodyguard opens the window on his side. "Ha! You also seem to have reached the end of the road, old bitch!"

The prosecutor smiles. "Ha ha ha! Both are ready for the scrap yard!"

The granny approaches the bodyguard to the left of the limo. "Please, Sir" she says, "help me get my van to the side."

"Ha ha ha! No way."

A motorcycle screeches to a halt at the right side of the limo. It is driven by a well-built guy; on the seat behind him is a beautiful, slim blonde with hair down to her bottom with her hands around her friend's belly. "You bitch!" swears the motorcyclist. "Away with that trash!"

The blonde looks at the bodyguard and winks. "Good morning!"

"Good morning, good morning," replies the bodyguard spontaneously.

"Ask those people to push that crate to the side," says the prosecutor.

The bodyguard seizes the opportunity to turn to the blonde. "Please help that pathetic granny to move her bus to the side."

"Why don't you help?"

"We are policemen."

The blonde pulls her head back slightly. "Ooh!"

The bodyguard notices that she is scared. "Don't worry. We are body guards of a very important person who works in the federal court."

The blonde gets off the bike while the rider doubts whether he will do the same.

At the same time the old woman quickly pulls out a gun from underneath her ragged coat, the blonde does the same, pulling a revolver from under the armpit of her blue leather jacket.

The old woman shoots the bodyguard on her side of the limo in his forehead; the blonde on the other side does the same. Both quickly turn their guns at the prosecutor, who tries to protect his face with the morning edition of *Die Welt*. Four bullets send him to another world. The old woman shoots twice at the driver, who with his hands bent instinctively tries to protect his head, but it does not help. Within a few seconds *Operation Revenge* is complete.

The old woman rushes to the van, screaming to the bikers, "Alex, Bianca, go!"

The blonde jumps nimbly on the backseat of the motorcycle, shouting to the old woman, who is about to enter the driver's door of the van, "Gill, good hits!"

The son of a SS general, who has disguised himself as an old woman, waves his hand as a sign of approval. "Yours too. Now go!"

The motorcycle takes off and flies towards the Schulbezirk Park. The minivan follows him.

The Hague Mouse pushes a button on his remote control. The video-recorder stops the filmed episode.

Avdo raises the thumb of his right hand. "All honor to you. Congratulations!"

Bianca gets up from the couch. "You guys want some coffee?"

The Hague Mouse nods. "Yes!"

"Yes, please. Thank you," Avdo adds spontaneously.

The thirty-year-old woman, long and slender as an arrow, with dyed red hair to her bottom, dressed in a pink blouse and the shortest miniskirt in the world, leaves the salon and with her wiggling hips walks to the kitchen.

Full of desire Avdo watches her leave. The Hague Mouse sees it, but pretends not to have noticed it. "Beautiful, no?"

"Yes, yes! Fantastic movie. Only was it smart to film all that? Imagine that falling into the hands of the police!"

"Ha ha ha!" the Hague Mouse grins. "We are the police. But I don't mean the movie, you idiot. I'm asking you if you like my wife."

"She's beautiful. Thank God. But you don't think ..."

"That you will give her a turn?" adds the Hague Mouse.

Avdo stirs in his place. "Man, are you crazy! I'm your pal."

"David was your pal too."

Avdo's face turns red as a ripe tomato. He clears his throat. "Hmm! Hmm! Yes, that was really stupid of me."

"Avdo! I'm asking you, do you want to fuck my wife?" The Hague Mouse shouts unexpectedly.

"Sure man!" Avdo starts sweating.

"Ha ha ha!" The Hague Mouse grins.

"I swear it!"

"Wait, you primitive prick. You don't understand. I like watching and filming when she fucks others."

Avdo wipes the sweat from his forehead. "You must be joking!"

The Hague Mouse draws nearer to him. "Not at all!"

"I don't understand!"

40

"These are my weaknesses."

"You don't mean ..?

"That others fucked her," the Hague Mouse adds.

"Well, I would murder them all."

"But I'm not you."

*

The Hague Mouse slaps him in the face, the child totters and falls. "Stupid ass!"

The boy whines and points to his hand. "She bit me in my little finger."

"And then you strangled her."

"I didn't strangle her."

"But?"

"I only beat her with a stick."

"With Raab's baseball bat. Right?"

"Yes! But I didn't kill her. I swear you!"

"No! No!" chuckles the Hague Mouse."You just wanted to stroke her?"

The boy begins to cry again. "She really bit me and threatened to tell everything to the journalists."

"You're always threatened by everyone."

"But it's really true!"

The Hague Mouse grabs the boy by the hand and lifts him up. "You're sick. But don't worry, I'll take care of it again, but this is the last time."

The boy wipes his tears away with his hand. "I promise you."

The Hague Mouse taps him on the shoulder. "And now we'll go to the sex club. You left her there, right?"

The boy nods.

"We need to remove the corpse and then I'll drive you home. I'll arrange everything with your mother."

"But her friend saw us."

"When?"

"When Edit got in Raab's Rolls."

"Who is she?"

"I don't know her name; she goes to the same Huibregtse School as Edit."

"Here in my home town of Wassenaar?"

"Yes."

"Do they know who you are?"

"I'm not sure, perhaps Edit bragged to her."

"Don't worry! Edit is now with our dear Lord. I'll arrange it. Money solves all problems."

The Hague Mouse motions Avdo and Raab to bring the dead child with them. Both lift the body of the eleven-year-old long-haired blond girl, wrap it in a blanket and go out on the street. The Hague Mouse opens the trunk of a Rolls. Avdo and Raab throw the dead child in it as if it were a regular mailbag.

"Are you nuts?" cries the boy.

The Negro Raab grins with his pearly white teeth and strokes the boy on his head. "Ha Ha Ha! She feels no pain anymore."

Avdo closes the trunk and the Hague Mouse, Avdo and the kid get in the limo; Raab returns to the brothel. The Hague Mouse starts the engine and drives towards Wassenaar. He taps a number into his colossal cell phone, weighing at least seven kilos, that is built into the Rolls. He gets connected and says with a bossy voice, "Sim, you and Abe come right away to the villa. I'll be there in half hour. It's urgent."

"I need somebody who looks like the kid," says the Hague Mouse.

"Try the zoo," chuckles sex baron Sim.

"Get lost!"

Abe, the owner of the brothel where the child was slain, comes in. "I know somebody... but."

The Hague Mouse frowns. "What?"

"One hand washes the other, right?"

"No problem. Tell me."

"Make sure my brother is released from prison."

The Hague Mouse raises his hand as if he wants to deliver Abe a blow. "That is impossible for the time being."

"Then give him leave once a week."

"Once a month for three days, that is okay. You tell me."

"Agreed. I know a doorman. He's much older than the boy, but he looks like him."

"Like two drops of water," Sim adds.

The Hague Mouse agrees. "Okay. Send him right away. Let him browse at least an hour around the Huibregtse School."

Abe holds out his hands. "What should I tell him?"

"Tell him that there is a safe stacked with money in the school and that he should see how it can be broken into."

Sim raises both thumbs. "Hague Mouse, you're a genius!"

"I know! And now get to work."

Chapter 3

AIRCRAFT FALL FROM
THE SKY LIKE RAINDROPS

December 20, 1988

TOP SECRET

WACE*, Amsterdam

To the Office of the General Director of the CIA.
Washington D.C.

Dear Bill,

Tomorrow evening, December 21, a Pan Am passenger plane Boeing 747 – flight N739PA – which is scheduled to depart from London Heathrow airport at 18:25 PM, British time, for John F. Kennedy Airport in New York will be kidnapped by an international anarchist gang of terrorists called Titans.

There is a well-founded suspicion that this plane will meet the same fate as have many previous ones: the above-mentioned gang will rob the passengers and then blow up the plane.

Urgent request: Delay this flight and if possible arrest the members of this gang.

Their names and descriptions have been known to you for a long time.

Yours sincerely,

WACE General Director for Europe.

---

* World Atomic Counter-Espionage
* A special phone developed by Dutch engineer Ferdi Elsas with which can be hacked into any telephone system in the world, including the red phone in the White House, as described in Mitric's true crime and love story *The Golden Tip*.
* "Clairvoyance" on demand. An estherist is therefore someone able to "predict"

December 20, 1988

TOP SECRET

GENERAL DIRECTOR OF THE CIA
WASHINGTON D.C.

To the General Director WACE Europe

Amsterdam

DO NOT GET INVOLVED IN MATTERS THAT ARE NOT
WITHIN YOUR JURISDICTION.

Yours sincerely,
General Director of the CIA.

*

Gill opens the hatch of the Pan Am Boeing 747 and drops a bag into
the dark night. He gives a signal to his companions. The first one to
jump is Avdo, then Alex followed by Bianca and finally he himself.

All fly like arrows. Gill catches up with the bag and jumps on it
as it were a horse.

At a height of over 1000 feet Gill pulls the handle; the parachute opens. He is followed by other members of the anarchist terrorist brigade *TITANS* who are taking part in this criminal operation.

Some 75 feet above the ground, Gill slips from his 'horse'; the
bag flies faster than he does. Soon, he hears a thud as the bag hits
the snowy blanket of the Yorkshire Dales pasture about fifty miles
north of the city of Manchester. Immediately after, he safely lands
himself in the white snowy blanket. There follows a thump behind
him, and then two more. He sees that all the members of his group
have landed safely.

Gill deftly unplugs his parachute, takes off his gas mask and
oxygen tank and swiftly packs his parachute. He turns around and

immediately sees three figures coming his way. "Look for the bag!" he orders.

"I've already found it," replies Bianca dragging the bag.

"What now?" Avdo wonders.

Gill presses a button to illuminate his watch. It is exactly 19:00 hours.

"The bomb placed on board of the aircraft can explode at any moment. I hope that everything will be alright."

"Nearby is Stanford road! Let's go there," suggests Bianca.

"Our jeep is hidden in a farm there," adds Alex.

"Okay We'll stay there for a few hours. And then on to More-cambe," orders Gill.

"Our yacht is anchored at the Morecambe harbor," adds Bianca weightily.

"Exactly! Bernard has been there for a few days already with the 'FBI Lawyer'," Gill adds.

Chapter 4

TEXEL

The sky is clear and a soft wind blows, cooling all living beings from the unbearable heat. The island of Texel in the Kingdom of the Netherlands during these summer days is full of tourists but also of terrorists.

Texel offers a professional skydiving course, for those who can afford it. The price is high, but the setting is magical.

The Hague Mouse has hired from his friend, the Prime Minister of the Netherlands, the best Air Force instructors from the Department of Defense to train his men.

Skydiving instructor, Colonel Van Noort, surrounded by dozens of beginner students, shows how to pack a parachute. "After you've jumped and successfully landed, make sure you immediately pack your parachute. Don't forget that it depends on you whether your parachute on another occasion opens, because ninety-nine percent of the accidents are caused by the wrong packing of your predecessors who had landed safely and consequently become "murderers" of their colleagues due to this deficient packing."

Avdo grins. "Man, why does not every one of us get their own parachute?"

Colonel Noort smiles. "That you will get when the training is completed, because there are no private parachutes here. So take care that the parachute with which you'll dive later is packed well."

"Hey man, you don't mean to say that I will jump with a parachute packed by someone else?"

"Not only you, but everyone."

Avdo begins to sweat, but this time not from the heat. "Well then I will jump with a parachute that I choose for myself."

47

"Agreed." The colonel continues packing the parachute and then to unpack it. "Okay, Bosnian, go ahead, pack this in the same way that I showed you."

Avdo kneels and packs the parachute neatly.

The colonel smiles contentedly. "Excellent! Now unpack it."

"Why, man!"

"So that others in turn can pack. Got it?"

"Yeah, yeah!"

Once they have all shown that they can pack the parachutes, and some even a couple of times, Colonel Van Noort points to a hangar. Now we're going to board the plane!"

Avdo butts in again. "Where are our parachutes?"

The Colonel laughs and in flawless Serbian says, "In the plane, man. But you don't need a parachute."

"Why is that?"

The colonel hugs him. "I'm kidding, man. I'll tell you a joke about a Bosnian parachutist when we take off."

The plane takes off from the runway and flies slowly towards the sea. Soon it reaches a height of 6,500 feet. The pilot then makes a circle and returns to the island.

The colonel distributes a parachute to every skydiver and puts one on himself.

Avdo makes himself heard. "You promised that I could have your parachute."

The colonel begins to take off his parachute. "No problem."

"Ha ha ha! I'm joking, man."

The colonel smiles. "I knew it! And now I'll tell you the joke about the Bosnian parachutist, okay?"

All the skydivers nod. "Let's hear it!" Avdo says.

"A Bosnian bragged that he could jump from a height of 6,500 feet without a parachute down onto a concrete road at the airport, and as a matter of fact with his head on an ordinary handkerchief that he had in advance soaked in water."

Avdo laughs. "I know that joke!"

"Really?"

"Yes! But in Belgium they say that it was a Dutchman and in

Holland that it was a Belgian."

The colonel cast a questioning look at Avdo. "Are you sure it's the same joke?"

"Absolutely! The Belgian jumps down from the plane, his head touches the handkerchief and blood begins to spray in all directions. The Belgian gets up and angrily asks, 'Who's the asshole that squeezed the water out of my handkerchief?'"

Everyone laughs. The colonel hugs Avdo. "Yes, that's the joke, but I heard it in Croatia, where they told me it was a Bosnian."

"I believe you! We in Bosnia say it was a Croat."

Again, everyone laughs. From the speaker the voice of the pilot is heard, "Everyone ready?"

The colonel gets serious, "Come on boys and girls, follow me!"

The colonel is the first leap into the abyss, followed by Rudy, Gill, Schmidt, Rita, Dolf, Helga, Karl, Robert, Frida, Klaus, Fritz, Charles, Frank, Sigfried, Avdo, Alex and Bianca.

Chapter 5

TANZANIA

The plane makes a turn to the military airport Dodoma of the capital of the Federal Republic of Tanzania. At an altitude of 10,000 feet Rudy jumps first, followed by Gill, Schmidt, Rita, Dolf, Helga, Karl, Robert, Frida, Klaus, Fritz, Charles, Frank, Sigfried, Avdo, Alex and Bianca. The president of the Republic of Tanzania, surrounded by his ministers, is staring at the sky.

The parachutists are flying through the air like arrows. At a height of 6,500 feet all 17 members of the elite parachute brigade *MODERN GLADIATORS* grab each other's hands and form a circle in the air, then they let go again. Rudi, Jules, Schmidt, Rita and Bianca form the shape of the number two, the rest divided into three groups of four parachutists form zero's. Those following this air show on ground are all able to read the number 2000.

At a height of 3,300 feet all parachutists part again. Rudi unfolds a large national flag of the Federal Republic of Tanzania. Bianca, Helga and Frida grab a hold of the other three sides of the flag. The other parachutists form a large semi-circle above the flag. The president of Tanzania jumps up and starts to applaud; his ministers followed him faithfully and shout out excitedly.

At a height of 1,000 feet all skydivers open their parachutes at the same time and soon land safely on the ground. They quickly undo their parachutes and fold them up. They line up quickly in a row according to height, and hand in hand make a bow toward the stands. The Tanzanian president applauds, the others follow suit.

Shortly after, the president extends his hand to the Hague Mouse. "Congratulations!"

The Hague Mouse chuckles. "My boys are ready to teach your parachutists the same art for a modest amount."

The sturdy black man flashes with his pearly white teeth and taps him on the shoulder. "Money is no problem. Just tell me the amount. I'll be grateful to you all my life."

Chapter 6

COMPUTER PROGRAMMER

From the ground floor of a stately house sounds soft piano music performed by a Canadian who works there as the house manager.

'Mossadman', who acts as the chief manager, looks out of a window on the third floor onto the garden and sees three athletic, masked men scaling the six-foot high fence. They then walking toward the back entrance.

'Mossadman' breaks out in a sweat. He forgets that the doors are locked and that it is impossible for intruders to enter. Quickly he taps a number on his cell phone and gets connected immediately.

"Amsterdam police headquarters."

"Help! Three armed men are trying to break into the house."

From the cell phone sounds a high-pitched female voice. "Who are you?"

"That's none of your business."

"Sir, please calm down! Where are you now?"

"Herengracht 106, it's urgent. They'll murder us all. Hurry up, woman!"

"You are in Amsterdam?"

"No! On de moon. Of course in Amsterdam. Stop asking stupid questions, send help! Herengracht 106, Amsterdam!"

'Mossadman' disconnects and leans out the window. He sees the masked types sliding something in the lock. He trembles with fear as a branch in the wind.

A dozen police cars with sirens blaring and lights turning stop in front of the entrance. With guns in their hands a couple of police-men run up the steps.

MI6 agent Sandor, who works there as a doorman opens the

door. Surprised, he looks around. The police officers push him aside and storm inside.

The house manger stops playing the piano. "Gentlemen, what can I do for you?"

"Where are the terrorists?" shouts one of the policemen.

The Canadian shrugs his shoulders. Several police officers rush up the stairs to the second floor. With a powerful karate kick, one of the policemen hits the office door of the business owner. The door collapses. Sitting upright on a luxury leather armchair behind a desk 'Englishman' stares in amazement at the newcomers. With his thumb he had closed one nostril. In the second nostril he had inserted one end of a rolled-up bill of 1000 guilders, while the other end was directed to a white line on a marble plate on which, besides a few other white lines, lie a gold razor blade and a large plastic bag with white powder.

*

The three-story house at Amsterdam's Herengracht 106 was bought by 'Englishman' for a few million dollars. He is hiding in Amsterdam, because the 'Jewish mafia' in San Francisco has blackmailed him; at least that is what he told his closest friends.

The 'English' millionaire amassed his fortune by selling patented computer programs to the U.S. Army. It was claimed that he was the best computer programmer in the world. In fact, all programs were developed by brilliant GRU engineers from the Soviet Union, programs he received via secret mail. In that way he built up the 'immune system' of the U.S. Army.

In fact, he 'sold' 'his' programs for $ 40 million each to a 'Jewish David' from San Francisco, the same programs that he already had sold for an even larger amount to the American government.

It seems that he had received that money so that he could disappear from America for a while, because the GRU had learned through a double agent in 'The White House' that on behalf of a certain 'World Atomic Counter-Espionage Service' the FBI had launched a secret investigation into 'Englishman's real identity.

That 'David' was in fact the GRU General Yuri Smolinski. 'Englishman knew that 'David' would not tell on him, because Smolinski knew that 'Englishman' was also a Russian, who had assumed the identity of an Englishman living previously in Australia, who had been sent prematurely to heaven by his Russian colleagues in an 'automobile accident', thus enabling 'Englishman' to adopt the identity of the poor beggar. But now that the case was leaked, he had became afraid because in America the electric chair for espionage and 'state treason' was awaiting him, or at best, the fate of the person whose identity he had successfully carried over the last twenty years.

By daily snorting high doses of cocaine he has turned his mental condition into a chronic state of paranoia, so that in each person he sees an FBI agent out to track him down and arrest him.

Chapter 7

"I am that terrorist!"

In the first century A.D. Roman imperialists conquered the city Vidovgrad and renamed it Akuincum. This city was built by the invading Celts from the north on the ruins of the city that the indigenous inhabitants of this extensive flat Serbian province had built and that the Celts had set on fire and razed to the ground. Their new city the Celts called Odube.

Vidovgrad (Akuincum) was until the fourth century the capital of the northern Serbian province of Pannonia. On the other side of the wide, sky-blue Danube rose the second Serbian city that the Serbs displaced to this side of the river built and that they called Perungrad. When this city was occupied by the wild Celts, they named it counter-Akuincum, because the Serbs from that city had begun a counter-revolution against the first invaders and after that the succeeding ones. In the seventh century, the Serbs succeeded again in recapturing their entire province of Pannonia and to restore the names of the cities according to their original gods. However, many protested against this, because in the first century many Serbs had converted to Christianity and therefore they believed that their cities ought to be named after their new saints.

In the 9th century, the Serbian province of Pannonia was occupied by the barbaric Hungarians, who founded the Kingdom of Hungary thereby renaming the cities from Perungrad Vidovgrad to Budim and Pest.

Thereafter in the year 1241, the wild Mongolian hordes, who belonged to the same race as the Huns and who in their trail even overpowered them, set the two Serbian towns on the Blue Danube

55

on fire, because Mongolians believed that cities bring forth evil. They stuck to their usual nomadic life in tents and since they rarely stayed long in one place, they soon left northern Serbia.

The Hungarians quickly regrouped and forced the occupied Serbs anew to rebuild the ruined cities, which were again given the names of Pest and Budim. From 1247 to 1341 Budim (Perungrad), where a big royal castle was built, served as the capital of the Kingdom of Hungary.

The invading Turks, who already in the 14th century had conquered almost the entire Serbian Empire and who had changed the capital of the new Serbian faith Tsar-City (Constantinople) in the ugly name Istanbul, continued their conquest to the last northern Serbian territory, the province of Pannonia and in the 16th century possessed almost the whole of so-called Hungary.

When Vidovgrad (Pest) fell in 1526, the Turks drove all the Serbs to the other side of the Danube, to Perungrad (Budim) Thereafter the development of Vidovgrad was forever stunted.

The Turks conquered the Serbian Perungrad (Budim) only after 1641; this year 41 will later prove to be a disastrous year for the Serbs and their cities. Perungrad (Budim) became a vizier city of the Turkish occupier, which was regularly maintained, while Vidovgrad (Pest) was razed to the ground. The Turks allowed no further construction of the town, fearing that the Serbs would again regroup and liberate their entire realm.

In 1686 Habsburg rulers conquered Vidovgrad (Pest). After that the Turks chased the remaining Serbs to the other bank of the Danube. In the falsified and politicized history of this period the pseudo professors and Germans call this "the migration of the Serbs in 1690". It is said that because of the Turkish oppression a priest called Arsenij Carnojevic moved with the unfortunate Serbs to the north. However, this is total nonsense! For this can only be called deportations of the Serbs from the occupied southern Serbian province to the north of Serbia, where from the beginning of this world only the peaceful and hospitable Serbian people lived, who throughout the ages, beginning with the Romans, Hungarians, wild Germans and brutal Turks were systematically extirpated, so that finally a very

small number of this oppressed people in the north of Serbia sur-
vived, now reduced to the small town of Taban in so-called Budim
city.

Vidovgrad (Pest) was from 1723 the royal center of the new
occupiers, which from the 18th to the 19th century grew very rapidly.

The Habsburg rulers or rather the Austro-Hungarian Empire
combined both cities in administrative governance. The population
increased rapidly, because the occupiers housed in that area of the
Serbian Empire all those who were not members of the Serbian race
and had no Serbian blood flowing in their veins. As a result even the
Serbs do not know now that these cities once belonged to them.
Vidograd and Perungrad (Budin-Pest) in 1900 had a population of
more than 730,000 thousand souls, during this period the Germans
settled more than 200,000 thousand Jews there.

In the First World War genocide took place on more than one mil-
lion indigenous people in northern Serbia - pure Serbs, excluding
the victims of the two million inhabitants in southern Serbia, while
in the Second World War, again many were slain in northern Ser-
bia, so-called Hungary and on the Balkans. During the Second
World War, 90 percent of the Jews in Vidograd and Perungrad
(Budin & Pest) were liquidated.

With their siege and daily bombardment, the Russians in 1944
almost destroyed all of Vidovgrad and Perungrad (Budin-Pest).

At present Vidovgrad Perungrad (Budin-Pest) is the official capital
of Hungary. Nobody mentions the Serbs, who day in and day out are
losing all their provinces and cities. After the dismantling of the
Soviet Union and the Warsaw Pact, the population of Vidov-
Perungrad (Budin-Pest) declined significantly to only half a million
people.

*

Today marks the festive opening of an international exhibition of
nearly all the famous old masters in the National Museum of Vidov-
Perungrad (Budin-Pest). Large posters of Rembrandt adorn the

57

entrance to the museum.

The opening ceremony is attended by many guests from around the world.

"I bet it was painted in Hong Kong!" jokes a prince from the United Arab Emirates, standing in front of a portrait of the Dutch painter Rembrandt.

"Bin, in your eyes everything is fake," teases Nick, one of his colleagues from the U.S. Secret Service.

"What does it matter whether it is an original or a forgery. Important is that it is beautiful," notes KGB colonel Boris Kulikov.

A 5 feet 11 tall, slim long-haired blonde points to the door with the words: *Private, do not enter. Admission restricted to museum personnel.*

"Gentlemen, please follow me. You are the last ones."

A dozen mysterious men disappear through the door opening. The blonde locks the door behind them. They walk up a marble staircase and at the top stop in front of another closed door. The blonde opens the door, allowing them to pass one by one into a large anteroom. She closes the door behind her and points ahead. Standing in front of a huge double doorway with gold fittings are two colossal figures dressed in civilian clothes and armed with machine guns at the ready. The blonde walks with her wiggling hips toward them. The company follows her. The guards open the door and everyone enters a large hall. The doors are closed behind them.

The hall looks like an old theater from the 18th century; beautiful balconies adorned with gilded carvings and statues of angels. The hall is full of guests sitting on plush, dark red seats.

The blonde walks to the front row and gestures to the vacant seats. When everyone is seated, the blonde bows and stands aside.

A half gray, old-looking man climbs with difficulty onto the podium that is decorated with gilded walls. He walks to the microphone placed in the middle of the podium.

"Dear friends, welcome! This is the first secret international anti-terrorism conference, a historic gathering. I know that you asked to be welcomed by the newly elected Director-General of WACE. Unfortunately he is unable to attend, but he asked me to extend greetings to you in his name."

There arises a loud grumbling in the hall. "He's always prevented," says someone. Others laugh.

The speaker covers his lips and clears his throat. "Hmm! Hmm! Like I said, this is a historic meeting. Due to the fact that the Soviet Union has ceased to exist, we now have the opportunity to fight together, shoulder to shoulder, against a common enemy: international terrorism. Until yesterday we were each other's enemies; that is being exploited by brutes from our camp as well as yours. Today we must shake hand in the spirit of reconciliation and jointly eradicate all those who are out to destroy whatever camp. We are aware that from a political standpoint there are many differences between us, but there are also common interests. Yes, despite differences in political views, we must prevent inhuman beings from playing us off against each other, or even, God forbid, start a Third World War. And we realize that there will be no winners then. Again, thank you all for coming here. You are welcome. Thank you. Hurrah!"

From the hall sounds generous applause. Everyone stands up and continues clapping. The blonde climbs on the podium to help the gentleman climb down. Then she returns to the microphone, takes it in her hand and stands to the left of the podium.

The screen displays a picture of Washington. An enormous Boeing crashes with its nose down on the Senate chamber of the Capitol.

Through the speakers sounds the soprano voice of the beautiful blonde. "Terrorists are planning on December 31, 1999 exactly at midnight to attack the U.S. Senate with airplanes."

Noises are heard from the audience. "Nonsense," someone shouts.

On the screen appears an image of the White House in Washington. A large plane crashes with its nose down on the building.

From the speakers sounds again the voice of the beauty. "The terrorists are also planning to attack this target at the same time."

Then new images appear. Manhattan in New York appears. Two huge Boeings crash into the Twin Towers.

"The terrorists plan," explains the speaker, "to raze both Twin Towers of the World Trade Center to the ground."

"Fairy tales for children!" someone shouts from the audience.

Many laugh, "Ha ha ha ..."

On the screen, the picture changes. An enormous Boeing crashes nosedives into the building of the UN.

"The United Nations will not be spared either," adds the blonde.

From the audience a voice is heard again: "Ha ha ha! Complete nonsense!"

Someone else calms him out loud. "Psst! Wait, man! Let her finish and then give comments."

The screen displays a nuclear plant with a large Boeing crashing down on it.

"The terrorists want to attack several nuclear power plants in the United States and Russia," the blonde goes on to explain.

Now there is excitement in the hall. Everyone looks at each other.

"Martians no doubt," someone yells out. "Who dreams up such baloney?"

Another voice interrupts him. "Keep your mouth shut, man!"

"Who said that? To me!?"

"Yes, to you! What do you want?"

"Boys, be quiet please!" a third voice says sternly.

The screen displays a new image: an enormous Tupolev nosediving into the central building of the Kremlin.

"The terrorists want on December 31 at midnight Moscow time to attack the Kremlin."

On the screen appears London, then Paris, The Hague, Frankfurt, Vatican City, Mecca. All photographs show again huge aircraft attacking these cities.

"The terrorists plan at the same time to cause a Boeing to crash on the MI6 building in central London, a Concorde on the Eiffel Tower in Paris, a Boeing on the Dutch Parliament in The Hague, the Central Bank in Frankfurt, the Vatican, Mecca ... "

The hall is now in an uproar. Some yell, "Who's that man, the terrorist who appears on all those photos?"

"Yeah! Yeah! Who is he?" many shout.

A man from the front row gets up and climbs onto the podium.

Through the speaker sounds again the voice of the blonde. "In all these collages the U.S. Secret Service Colonel Nick can be seen. You all know his legend well. The rest will be explained by our colleague Nick himself."

The blonde dressed in a miniskirt with high heels walks with her wobbly hips to an athletically built man of average height, dressed in a leather pilot jacket with a white hat and a close-cropped moustache. She puts the microphone back on the stand.

The man in the white hat takes advantage of the occasion. "A little kiss perhaps?"

The blonde embraces him, kisses him on the cheek and leaves the podium.

"Bravo!" someone shouts from the audience.

The man in the white hat comes closer to the microphone, holds the stand with one hand and with the other takes off his hat. "Dear colleagues, I'm that terrorist!"

A deadly silence ensues in the hall.

Chapter 8

WHITE INDIANS

Amsterdam Ruigoord is as always full of visitors. There is an old church building and a large theater that doubles as a restaurant when there are no performances. Almost all known Dutch cabaret singers, musicians and actors began their careers here.

Not far from the theater is a real Indian camp with teepee tents and a large campfire burning night and day. Indian warriors armed with spears and bow and arrow give demonstrations to the public in the art of archery.

The chief with a headdress of artificial eagle feathers on his head is sitting cross-legged in front of his teepee. Beside him on a chair sits a gentleman dressed in a black Kangol suit and a white shirt with a perfectly knotted red tie. He is wearing a black hat that hides his balding head.

Surrounded by young Indian girls the chief smokes a peace pipe. A Dutch girl dressed up as an Indian squaw, seductively swaying her hips, serves the chief and his important guest tea that gently simmers in a copper kettle in fresh leaves of peppermint and marijuana that the white Indians grow in the heart of Amsterdam.

The chief hands the pipe to his guest. "Sir, take a puff or two!"

The Hague Mouse bows politely. "Thank you, but I don't smoke hash."

"Man, this is first class marijuana. Made in Amsterdam."

The Hague Mouse shakes with his hand. "I don't smoke at all."

The Canadian dressed up as an Indian chief does not give up. "Take one puff! You don't need to inhale."

The boss of the modern gladiators takes a puff, immediately blows out the smoke and gives back the pipe. "Are you happy now?"

"Absolutely. Many eyes are watching us. Now they'll believe that you're one of us."

"Oh! Now I understand."

After a while the chief stands up and points to the entrance of his teepee. "Come to my office, sir. There we can do business in peace."

"Can you adopt twenty warriors into your tribe?" asks the Hague Mouse.

The Canadian spreads his hands. "That depends!"

"On what?"

"First, how much you pay. And second, I want to know what's it all about."

"Money is not the problem. But what it's about is none of your business."

"Then no."

"You know who I am, don't you?"

"So what?"

"You seem to forget that the beautiful man from The Hague has put a million guilders on your head. Imagine if it leaks that you're hiding here behind fake eagle feathers?"

The Canadian clears his throat. "Um hmm! I heard that, but I haven't squealed on him."

"I know. But he doesn't know; eight years in prison is no joke."

"I had nothing to do with it."

"I know! But you knew what he was doing then. He is convinced that it's all your fault. After all, your Canadian colleagues of the CSIS have broken his neck."

"I have nothing to do with."

"Well I told you, I know. But be a little wiser. It's better that way."

"I don't understand ..."

The Hague Mouse takes a pile of money from the inside pocket of his coat. "Why it is necessary for my men to be adopted in your tribe is none of your business. I think one hundred thousand guilders are enough for a start, yes?"

The blue eyes of the Canadian flash the flame of newly lit

match. He stares at the money. "Do you promise that I won't end up in the shit?"

The Hague Mouse gives him the money. "Of course! Indeed, even they don't know what they're being prepared for."

"How long must they stay with me?"

"One or two months."

"And then?"

"Then you send them to your chief."

"In Canada?"

"Yes!"

"How long?"

"One or two years."

The Canadian thinks for a moment. "That'll cost you a pretty penny."

"No problem."

"Something else."

"Tell me."

"They should all follow the rules of the tribe."

"Of course."

"You don't understand."

"What?"

"Immediately after they've been taken up into my tribe, their heads should all without exception, boys and girls, be shaved bald."

"Well, that's no problem. They're all professionals."

The chief puts the money in his bosom."Then it's a deal."

Chapter 9

FATEFUL FLIGHTS

The Boeing takes off from the runway and soon reaches its cruising altitude of 33,000 feet.

The pilot's voice recommending his airline can be heard from the loudspeakers: "Good morning everyone! I am your Captain John. We have successfully climbed above the clouds. This morning the weather is clear over the cap that Boston is wearing. All kidding aside, as you know, we're flying in the direction of the most beautiful city in the world, Los Angeles. Our charming hostesses will be happy to serve anything you want. Please feel free to order, the first drink is obviously at the expense of American Airlines. Release your seat belts, stretch yourselves a little and enjoy the flight."

The captain signs off.

Several flight attendants start serving the passengers at once.

An athletic black-haired passenger waves to a stewardess whose hair almost reaches to her bottom.

She approaches him. "Good morning! What can I do for you?"

The black-haired passenger smiles. "A lot. But let's start with a vodka martini."

"So early?"

"Ah! I've been up for a long time."

The stewardess looks at him and smiles. "Are you sure?"

He understands what she's driving at. "How do you know that I am a Muslim?"

"That's what I suppose.".

"You guessed right. But I'm not very religious. Are you a Muslim?"

"Oh, no! My mom is an American."

"And your father?"

"Chinese!"

"These are the most beautiful women in the world ... At least that is what we Egyptians think, and you are proof that I'm not wrong."

The stwardess smiles and moves to fetch the order.

*

Three figures in the baggage compartment in the belly of the plane scramble out of a big box and quickly put on parachute suits and parachutes, and then draw special gas masks over their faces.

Schmidt looks at his watch, it is exactly 8.15 am. He nods to his colleagues that it's time for action. They move up to another compartment. Rita deftly opens the cap of an oxygen tube. The tube is connected to the cabin and other parts of the aircraft. Dolf inserts a plastic hose from a metal five liter-bottle into the mouth of the tube. Then he opens the valve of the bottle, the Czech sleeping gas begins to sizzle ...

Schmidt once again glances at his watch, it is 20 minutes past eight. He gives a signal with his hand to move upward. All three of them climb out of the baggage compartment and enter the passenger's cabin.

All passengers have already fallen asleep in a heavenly dream world. Schmidt jumps over the flight attendant with long black hair – beside her on the floor lies an empty glass – and proceeds to the cockpit. His colleagues begin to search the passengers, taking their precious jewelry, removing their purses and putting everything in their backpacks.

Schmidt attaches an object to the front door of the cockpit and steps back a few yards. Then he hides behind the partition separating first and second class. He removes a device from his pocket presses on it. There is a small explosion and the door is opened. Schmidt hurries inside. Both pilots are also in a dream world.

Schmidt takes a minicomputer from his backpack and connects the accompanying cables to the appropriate contacts situated above the body of the co-pilot. In the course of his action, he pushes the co-pilot aside in order to place the minicomputer on the table. He then taps something into the computer. The plane began to fly towards Canada, but soon bends and sets course for New York City.

Satisfied with the work done, Schmidt leaves the cockpit.

THE FIRST TEAM

Schmidt opens the hatch of the aircraft. At a height of 33,000 feet he jumps head first into the abyss, followed by Rita and Dolf. They plummet down like arrows. All three breathe oxygen from special tanks. Far below them lies a dense cloud cover. In dozens of seconds, the trio is lost in water vapor. Immediately afterwards they see vast plains.

At a height of less than 1000 feet Schmidt pulls the handle. The parachute opens. His friends follow him. Soon all three successfully hit the dry grass.

All untie the parachutes and pack them in. They take off their backpacks and their parachute overalls, which they had put over their street clothes.

Schmidt produces a small military shovel and quickly digs a hole. Rita and Dolf do the same. Within minutes, they bury their parachutes and equipment.

Schmidt draws a cell phone from his leather pilot jacket and taps a number. Immediately he gets connected. Although they are far from any inhabited area, he whispers, "Hello! Black eagle here"

"Are you all right!"

"Yes! All three of us are alive and well."

"Nobody saw you!"

"Nobody!"

"Okay! Good luck."

"Thanks!"

The three of them walk towards a highway.

*

The modified Boeing 767-200, American Airlines Flight 11, flies toward New York.

A transmitter sends out signals.

The computer in the plane responds by decreasing its altitude. Underneath the aircraft appear tall buildings. The computer further reduces its altitude to 1000 feet.

The roar of the low flying plane causes New Yorkers to look up.

A taxi driver peers through his side window. Waving a clenched fist, he yells out, "The route of the pilot is not normal. The building will get hit!"

His customer looks at the sky. "Maybe the pilot's drunk."

At exactly 46 minutes after 8 o'clock, the nose of the Boeing 767-200, in which 200 kg. of high-grade uranium was hidden, hits the North Tower of the World Trade Center at full speed, exactly at the office where the transmitter was located. Immediately there is a strong explosion and then the fuel tank explodes in turn, causing a huge fire that spreads at lightning speed. All government employees on that floor are instantly burned alive.

Panic arises throughout the tower. People run toward the elevators and through emergency exits into the stairwells. They push and shove each other. Women are screaming hysterically and falling down on the marble floors. Men are trampling them. Everyone wants to vacate the building as quickly as possible.

New Yorkers on the street look up at the huge fireball in stunned silence. Black smoke rising into the air seems to have returned from the days when the natives of the newly discovered continent sent smoke signals.

The taxi driver hits both hands on the steering wheel. "What did I tell you!"

His customer nods! "Yes! Yes! Unfortunately, you were right!"

THE FOURTH TEAM

Helga opens the hatch of the aircraft. At a height of 33,000 feet she jumps head first into the abyss, followed by Karl and Robert. They plummet down like arrows. All three breathe oxygen from special tanks. Far below them lies a dense cloud cover. In dozens of seconds, the trio is lost in water vapor. Immediately afterwards they see vast planes.

At a height of less than 1000 feet, Helga pulls the handle. The parachute opens. Her friends follow her. Soon all three successfully hit the dry grass.

All untie the parachutes and pack them in neatly. They take off their backpacks and parachute overalls, which they had put over their street clothes.

Helga produces a small military shovel and quickly digs a hole. Robert and Karl do the same. Within minutes, they bury the parachutes and their equipment.

Helga takes a cell phone from her leather pilot jacket and taps a number. Immediately she gets connected. "Hello!" she whispers. "Black eagle number 4 here."

"Are you all right!"

"Yes!"

"No one saw you!"

"No! What about the other birds?"

"One has successfully found the nest."

"Excellent! What now?"

"Act according to instructions."

"Okay! Bye!"

"Good luck."

THE THIRD TEAM

"Hello! Black eagle number 3 here."

"Are you all right!"

"Yes!"

"No one saw you!"

"No! What about the other birds."

"First Eagle scored a hit!"

"Bravo Gill!"

From the speaker of the phone sounds a hoarse voice. "Bitch! Don't mention my name!"

"Sorry! I'm excited."

"We'll talk about that later. The fourth eagle died in flight."

"How's that?"

"We don't know. Follow the instructions."

"Will do! Don't worry!"

"Good luck!"

The threesome walk toward a highway.

The modified Boeing 757, United Airlines Flight 93 flies on toward Washington. Suddenly the plane is hit by a rocket. The plane plummets. Within seconds the nose of the plane, in which 200 kg. of high-grade uranium was hidden, hits the ground. Big explosions are echoed. The plane explodes into a hundred pieces. Two F-15 fighter jets fly over the downed aircraft.

From the speaker of the first jet sounds a happy voice. "Good shot Lisa."

"Thanks Bill!"

THE SECOND TEAM

The modified Boeing 767, United Airlines Flight 175, is heading for New York.

The transmitter sends out signals.

The computer in the Boeing reduces the altitude. Underneath the aircraft appear skyscrapers. The computer reduces the altitude again to 1000 feet.

New Yorkers on the street look up and shout in chorus, "Oh my God! Not again!"

At exactly 3 minutes after 9 'o clock, the nose of the Boeing, in which 200 kg. high-grade uranium was hidden, slams at full speed into the South Tower of the World Trade Center, exactly at the office where the transmitter was located. A huge explosion follows. Immediately, the fuel tank explodes, causing a huge fireball that spreads at lightning speed. All employees on that floor are also instantly burnt alive.

New Yorkers are looking up in stunned silence at the inferno. Black smoke from both towers rises into the air.

The taxi driver and his customer step out of the cab. "Wow, this is no coincidence, I tell you! This is a terrorist attack."

"Yes! Yes!" His customer nods. "You're damn right!"

Chapter 10

"This is only a conventional rocket. Do you want war? You tell me!"

Gill taps a number in the Elsas phone[*] and gets connected. "We have a problem."

"Explain!" replies the Hague Mouse through the same type of phone.

"Five eagles were killed in the air, only two have successfully reached the nest."

"How is that possible?"

"No idea."

"What now?"

"Dragonflies"

There is a short pause. Then the Hague Mouse says, "Only one. Direction spiders nest."

"With or without the sting?"

"Without."

"As you like."

"And of course let Mr. Delirium call that cowboy asshole 'personally'."

"Don't worry."

The call is disconnected.

Gill activates a special computer program, for which the Hague Mouse has paid a fortune to the "Englishman", the computer programmer. The screen displays a schematic representation of U.S. military satellites. Gill begins to browse in a manual and then taps

_____

[*] A special phone developed by Dutch engineer Ferdi Elsas with which can be hacked into any telephone system in the world, including the red phone in the White House, as described in Mitric's true crime and love story *The Golden Tip*.

some codes. A dot on the screen starts flashing. Gill browses further. Soon he finds what he needs, and again taps something on the computer. The screen divides into two parts. One part is the already activated satellite schema, on the other part appears the geographical map of America and Cuba. Gill taps another code. In the second half a dot starts to flash, after which the text appears "Aircraft Carrier George Washington". First whispering to himself and then exclaiming *Yes!* Gill presses another special key. After a short while, the dot starts moving toward Cuba. Again he taps something on the computer. The screen is now divided into three parts. The new panel shows a map of the capital of America. He looks quickly in the manual and starts typing the code of one of the five previously installed receivers that now, for some reason, the planes have failed to reach. There too a dot starts blinking and the text "PENTAGON" appears. Gill again taps something on the computer. The dot that was moving fast toward Cuba now changes direction and returns full speed toward Washington.

Gill rubs his hands in satisfaction. "You imperialist motherfuckers," he says to himself. "Here's something you didn't expect!"

He takes the Elsas phone in his hand and types a few letters. The display shows a name. Gill counts a few numbers out loud and through the speaker sounds the voice of the President of Russia, "Yes!"

Among shouts of joy, he again taps a number and gets connected. De voice at the other end says, "Dick Cheney!"

Gill is surprised; this is not what he had expected. Clearly, he had entered from the phone number of the President of Russia the number of the red phone of the President of the United States. Soon he recovers himself. "Ah, oh, Dickey boy! Is that you there?"

In the anti-nuclear bunker where Dick Cheney immediately after the first attack by the airplane in New York has set up headquarters a deathly silence prevails. After a while, Gill hear the anxious voice of the Vice President of America, "I don't understand!"

"Listen, Dickey boy, give my greetings to Cowboy George. This is only a conventional rocket. Do you want war! You tell me!"

Gill disconnects. "Yes!" he says to himself.

Chapter 11

"Bin Laden is the terrorist behind 9/11."

In the anti-nuclear bunker deep beneath the White House all members of the cabinet as well as the heads of intelligence and counterintelligence have come together.

The president nervously bites his lower lip. "National Security claims that the telephone call did not come from Moscow!"

The National Security Agency director nods. "That's a thousand percent!"

The vice president spreads his arms. "People! I recognized his voice ... "

The NSA Director begins to explain."Mister President, there is no doubt that it is not so. But recently a special phone has been developed that can simulate all of our voices."

Everyone looks at each other, dumbfounded.

"Why have we not been informed of this in time?" demands the president of the United States angrily.

"The head of the NSA clamps his lips together. "That you should ask those who are above us."

"What? I am the president!"

"Yes, you are, George," smiles the Secretary of Defense, "but only on paper. You and all of us. The rocket that destroyed the General Staff of Counter Intelligence at the Pentagon was fired from our aircraft carrier! "

Again a deadly silence ensues.

After a while, the President stammers, "Wwelll ... nnoww, that mmeans.."

The CIA director completes his train of thought. "That we can destroy ourselves."

"Are there any alternatives?"

A mysterious, small stocky and balding man, who has remained silent up to this point, takes a stack of documents out of his briefcase and spreads the papers out on the table. All those present pick up a copy.

"Yes there is, George! Take note of this: today you will inform the Senate that behind all these attacks is bin Laden."

The president of America reads for himself the content of the document and blows through his lips. "Ppaperrr! Who will believe this nonsense?"

"Everyone! George, everyone! It all depends on you. Gentlemen, I hope you will be wise enough."

Chapter 12

TITANS

September 11, 2007

It is the dead of night and pouring rain. In the distance, flashes of lightning can be seen and crashing sounds of thunder heard. The wind has reached the velocity of a storm and the waves are splashing onto the deck of the ship that is making some 10 knots an hour.

Suddenly the voice of the captain is heard. "Stop the engines!"

"Yes, sir!" the helmsman replies through the speakers. The ship slows down.

"We are there!" says the commander of the diving crew, Dutchman Hank.

"Are you sure?" the captain asks.

Hank places his forefinger on a particular spot on the map. "I'm absolutely sure. You see, here's the exact position of the underwater cave."

"Okay," the captain replies.

The ocean vessel "The New Mecca" stops. Tens of young men geared in modern underwater outfits jump from the boat down into the sea. Dutchman Hank jumps in last.

*

On the fifth floor of the former central command center of the Soviet Security Service, KGB, situated on Felix Drzinjski's square, nothing much has changed from the times that the Soviet Union ceased to exist as a result of the Cultural Revolution based on the Gorbachev doctrine. The same room no. 1007 still houses the headquarters of the Russian "Wet Works".

"You must leave for Amsterdam right away," says Vladimir

Bachirev, handing Colonel Boris Kulikov a big envelope.

"Very well, sir." Boris salutes like a soldier even though wearing civilian clothes: a black leather jacket, American jeans, genuine American boots, and sporting a cap with the words "I Love NY" on it.

"Don't forget to give my greetings to Walter," adds the general, tapping Boris on the shoulder. "He lives temporarily in Amsterdam now. You'll find his address in this envelope. And bring me back that bag of diamonds. He will also give you a platinum VISA card with the same name on as the last time."

"Yes sir," replies Boris. He leaves the office.

*

"I have a match with Denis today," says Tina.

"Denis the Penis," replies Amnon.

Tina's face becomes red as a tomato; she bites her lips and gets angry. "Oh, you are so jealous!"

"Nonsense! Me jealous at that shitty Jew!" Amnion shouts.

"You anti-Semite!" she yells back.

Amnon stops for a second. "I'm not an anti-Semite."

"Yes you are!"

"Why are you saying that?"

"Because you hate Denis just for being a Jew."

"I don't hate that arrogant Jew," he admits unexpectedly, "I'm just jealous of him."

"You're jealous of his amateur tennis. You're crazy."

He smiles. "Not of his tennis, stupid. But of his penis…"

"Oh, boys, boys," Tina sighs.

Tina is an extremely good-looking blue-eyed blond American girl, twenty-years old and five feet ten tall. Following the orders she received from HRT in San Francisco, she is temporarily living in the Netherlands and studying law at the University of Amsterdam. Twenty-one year old Amnon has curly dark hair, sapphire green eyes and towering more than six feet tall is an athletic type like some ancient Greek god. As commanded by the Mossad, he replaced Tel Aviv for Amsterdam, was given a new identity as "Mustafa" and now studies together with Tina at the same university. There they met and fell in love. Tina convinced Amnon to work for the United States and in his new identity as a refugee from Iran he accepted that offer gladly, playing his role of an anti-Semite so well that the devil himself would be jealous of him.

Amnon turns serious. "Did you get a call from Walter?"

"Mustafa!" Tina's face turns white as snow.

"What's wrong with you?" Amnon tries hugging her.

Tina slips out of his hands. "How many times do I have to tell you to be careful not to mention the real name of our boss?"

"Oh," he steps back. "But I'm only telling this to you and no-body else."

"Please, not even to me. Here in Amsterdam even the asphalt has ears, you idiot."

Amnon tries cracking a joke. "I'm so sorry, pretty miss! It won't happen again. I give you my honest anti-Semite word."

"Mustafa!"

"Tina!"

They look at each other and continue their conversation, whispering to one another, so silent that even the Amsterdam asphalt could not hear them.

*

The divers locate the entrance to the cave without any trouble. *It is in fact not simply a cave, but an underground and underwater secret bunker as well that, before being modernized, used to be for centuries in the hands of Arab pirates who used it as a hiding place to stash their fortune. Sometime in the mid-sixties of the 20th century, the Dutch mafia bought the cave, having made a special agreement with the Asian mafia to mutually collaborate with the Arab drug smugglers. From then on, they used the cave to hide tons of Asian heroin that was afterwards transferred onto the European and American black markets.*

The entrance is hidden masterly by a fake coral reef. The divers remove the coral and open the two-meter wide round polyester door. Hank explains to them that polyester was chosen as building material so that American hunters for underwater bombs would be unable to detect the cave. Behind the door, they perceive a dark long tunnel stretching out in front of them.

Hank enters first, the rest follow him. They dive for more than fifteen minutes. At the end of the upwards sloping tunnel, the divers emerge from the water and enter the dark cave. Hank turns on the aggregator. The lighting shows a cave the size of a football field, giving the divers who are here for the first time the impression of being in one of the stories from the Arabian "1001 Nights".

Everything is stored in this huge depot; next to a supply of fresh water there are tons of heroin, hashish, cocaine, amphetamines, ecstasy pills and thousands of Kalashnikov's, various pistols and revolvers, hand grenades and bombs, together with more than a million different bullets and rifles.

Hank shows them ten steel cylinders. "This is highly refined plutonium", he says proudly. "And these two rockets," pointing to two rockets three yards long, "are armed with a nuclear warhead. I myself took them out of that unlucky American plane that crashed into the sea near Naples."

"Real atom bombs," one of the divers, a Swede named Leif, says astonished.

"Yeah, real American nuclear bombs," Hank replies proudly.

*

A big white eight-door armored Mercedes halts in one of the streets near the canal overlooking Artis, the Amsterdam zoo. The driver gets out, lights a cigarette and starts looking around.

"Are you sure she will come?" Boris asks suspiciously.

"Absolutely sure," replies Walter calmly lighting the Monte Carlo cigar he had received that day from Arigato. He takes a deep breath, inhales the smoke and blows it on purpose slowly into Boris' face.

Boris starts to cough and tries to escape the smoke. "Are you crazy? You want me to get cancer?" Boris grumbles.

"Ha ha ha!" Walter laughs.

The driver knocks on the window. Walter presses on the button to open it.

"She's coming," the driver whispers.

"Okay," mumbles Walter.

A quite tall and red haired woman appears, slowly bicycling over the bridge leading to Sarphati Street

On her way to the parked limousine, she suddenly stops, jumps off her bike as from a horse and gives it to the driver to hold it for a minute. She looks around carefully, and after having made sure that nobody is following her, she takes out a small parcel from her bag. She approaches the car, salutes the occupants by placing her fist next to her temple and skillfully hands the parcel through the window. Then she takes her bike back and riding towards Kodekadijk Street disappears in the dark.

"That was Thea," Boris says.

"Oh, you already know each other," Walter says a little surprised.

"Yes, from the Cold War period. Her husband helped us liquidate Slayer in Switzerland."

"The weapons dealer?"

"No, her second husband."

"The anarchist?" Walter is still surprised.

"Yes. Tinus guaranteed for him."

"But what was the reason for eliminating Slayer?"

"Vladimir was convinced that Slayer was close to discovering the identity of Fichte."

"Slayer was Fichte?"

"Nonsense, Fichte is a woman."

"A woman?"

"Yes, a woman!"

"And that's how the Dutch Red Brigades did the job?"

"That's right. Nobody could have imagined even in their wildest dreams that the Dutch would liquidate Slayer."

"And we from the CIA believed that they worked for us and paid them so much money!"

"We are very grateful for that. Trust me, we are very grateful!"

"My God!" Walter breaks out in sweat.

"Leif!" Hank shouts. "We've have to take one of these rockets and two steel cylinders with plutonium with us."

"No problem," the Swede replies.

With much effort, five divers finally manage lifting the rocket armed with a nuclear charge. Slowly they put it into the water. Hank orders them to dive in front of him. Together with a diver, Leif lifts one steel cylinder and dives in. Hank and another diver take care of the other cylinder. Hank turns off the aggregate and all leave the cave in complete darkness. With the use of his flashlight, Hank locates the other diver. Both dive in and within ten minutes, the whole crew is back into the ocean. Hank orders them to close the entrance by replacing the big polyester lid and hiding it behind the fake coral reef. Hank then orders Leif to snorkel up to the surface to check if everything is safe. Together with the other divers, he remains underwater, awaiting the news.

*

"Captain! Captain!" somebody yells through the speakers.

"Yes! What is it?" the captain replies.

"A big destroyer is coming straight at us from starboard," the voice from the speaker answers.

The captain gazes through his binoculars and surveys the right side. He freezes immediately: the captain of "The New Mecca" clearly discerns a destroyer with a US flag approaching his ship.

"Everyone to their positions!" the captain commands through the speakers to the rest of his crew. "Stay calm and leave everything to me."

*

Leif snorkels up to the surface. Struck by what he sees, he stops breathing for a second. Right in front of him, less than fifty yards away, he spots a huge US destroyer positioned next to the freighter. He sees American soldiers boarding his ship.

Leif remains calm and snorkels back. Although swimming as fast as he can, he feels he is making as much speed as a turtle. In a couple of minutes, he gets back to his friends. Using his hands only, he motions to Hank and the rest what is going on.

Hank immediately removes the coral reef again with the help of his crew. They reopen the entrance quickly and enter the tunnel with the nuclear weapons. Hank remains behind together with Leif in order to close the polyester lid properly and to replace the coral reef. When having made sure that everything is in order, they start to swim as far away from the entrance as possible. After a few hundred yards, they find a small cave by accident. To their relief they discover that they have sufficient oxygen in their gas cylinders to remain alive for the next five hours.

*

"Just a routine check-up!" says the commander of the American Navy destroyer. "Please, allow my men to inspect your ship."

"Go ahead," replies the captain of *The New Mecca*.

The destroyer draws up to the freighter. Several fully armed soldiers jumped neatly onto the ship.

"Why have you dropped your anchor here?" the commander of the inspection team inquires.

"We had some problems with one of our engines. Our mechanics are doing their best to solve the problem as soon as possible," replies the captain.

The commander of the inspection team checks their documents and having made sure that everything is in order, he addresses the captain. "So, you're sailing to Rotterdam?"

"That's right. And then to New York."

"Can we check the inside of your ship?"

"Yes, please do as you like."

While the rest of the inspectors are searching the whole ship, their commander asks the captain of *The New Mecca* to follow him to the main engine room. Climbing down the stairs, he sees several mechanics working and sweating around one of the engines. Everything seems as it should. After more than half an hour, the inspectors finish their work and their commander orders them back to the destroyer.

"I hope you don't object to our divers inspecting the ship from below?" he asks the captain.

"Of course not."

The commander gives a sign to a special diving crew and ten of them dive into the ocean. A few of them check the ship, while two divers continue to the bottom of the ocean that was some fifty yards deep at the spot where the anchor was dropped. Having ascertained that everything seemed in order, the whole team surfaces again. A special crane picks them up from the sea and puts them back on their ship.

The commander says farewell to the captain of *The New Mecca*. "Everything is perfectly in order. I apologize for the disturbance, but we have to stick to our regulations."

"I understand completely," the captain replies. "During these times of increasing terrorism, I am very relieved that you are working for the safety of all of us."

The commander returns to his ship. The US destroyer parts slowly from *The New Mecca* and picking up speed sails away into the distance. Within a few minutes, both ships vanish into the dark rainy night.

Chapter 13

ESTHERISM[*]

In the bar of the Amsterdam Hilton, the heads of the world's two most powerful secret services are holding a secret meeting.

"The Hague Mouse is an estherist. We cannot trust him," says CIA director Bill Bennett.

"Estherist! What is that?" asks the director of the KGB, Vladimir Putin, surprised.

"An estherist is a man who has certain 'foreknowledge' that a terrorist attack or an assassination of a prominent figure, like a king or head of state, is about to happen; in fact he knows that in advance because he himself is the organizer of such actions."

"Where did you get that?"

"What?

"This doctrine or knowledge?"

"Our current director of WACE graduated in secret with a doctorate on this subject at the Arizona College of Police Science, when I was director of the FBI."

"Our common competitor? I'm curious."

"It includes among other things that estherists always operate 'in teams'. The estherist engages the assassin, who trusts him. He convinces the hit man that the act he has to carry out is a sacred thing and that if they expose him he must not reveal who engaged him. When the estherist has come so far, he engages informants who must attempt to elicit information from the killer about his plans. Then he tells the informants that it concerns a 'holy cause' and that this crime should be prevented, a crime that the estherist himself has

---

[*] "Clairvoyance" on demand. An estherist is therefore someone able to "predict" future events.

83

conceived. When he has managed to obtain irrefutable proof that the murderer or terrorist really intends to commit the crime, the estherist contacts the intended victim stating that his "conscience" and "love" for the victim cannot allow this crime to happen ... "

The CIA director takes his glass of whiskey from the table and takes a few sips.

His colleague gesticulates impatiently with his hand. "Please continue."

The Director of the Central Intelligence Agency puts his almost empty glass on the table. "By saving the victim from a 'certain death', all doors in his country are opened wide for the estherist. This 'expert' will become head of the secret services of the country where he 'saved' the life of the victim, so that the poor fellow and his country do indeed become victims ... "

"Interesting. How many estherists are there out there?"

"We don't know for sure, because not everyone can be a estherist, the discipline is confined to highly trained people who must outdo the greatest actors working for the 'perfect crime'."

"Can you guess at least who they are?"

"Yes! The WACE director has even suggested in 1986 that he keeps thinking of the Hague Mouse."

"And!?"

"The father of our current foolish top cowboy has put it down as complete nonsense."

"Of course, the Hague Mouse is his chief advisor."

"Where do you get that from!"

"He once boasted that to one of our double agents."

"In our official service?"

"No! In his own private service."

The CIA director shakes his head. "Now I understand everything. Thanks to his doing, criminology is not yet able to fight against estherism. Not yet, but I hope the time has come to think deeply about it."

"Together we'll probably manage."

"God help us! Otherwise we're lost."

END OF OPERATION TWINS PART TWO

APPENDICES

9/11 -
THE ACCUSATION

Appendix I – A Trial Run for 9/11?

On October 4, 1992 an Israeli El Al Boeing 747-258F transport plane crashed into two apartment blocks in the Bijlmer, a suburb of Amsterdam, claiming the lives of 43 people and many more wounded, excluding an unknown number of unregistered poor illegal third world immigrants. This may be far removed from the reference world of the average American reader, but this may change when he reads in the above text by Slobodan Mitric from p. 131 of *The Serbian Army*, Nr. 8, December 21, 1992 that he has been informed by a reliable source that none other than the same person indentified in this book as the mysterious The Hague Mouse also orchestrated this disaster: "The official explanation given by the Dutch and Israeli authorities is that the accident was caused by engines defects. Rumors will have it that it was a terrorist attack. I had to censor this article at that time, because the heading was, Terrorist Use Israeli Military Aircraft to Drop an Atomic Bomb on Amsterdam – 200 kilo's enriched plutonium were on board the plane that was transporting high-tech military cargo. A top official of the BVD [Dutch Internal Security Service] told me back then in confidence that it was a terrorist attack by The Hague Mouse..."

In the light of the above information the distinct possibility can therefore not be discounted that it was a trial-run for 9/11, with similar ingredients: a plane with nuclear material on board guided by a transmitter planted in its target.

Who's Afraid of The Hague Mouse?

Towards the end of the second chapter "Modern Gladiators" of this novel one of its main characters, albeit under an alias, is introduced: The Hague Mouse, an enormously influential, corrupt and affluent person with the power to mitigate prison sentences, intimately involved in an international secret pedophile network and, as mentioned, and who appears to be leading figure in the group behind the 9/11 attacks.

In this chapter, there is a reference to a doorman, who looks similar to a young boy-lover of The Hague Mouse, a boy who has just "by accident" killed a young girl in this pedophile network. This slightly older unnamed doorman can then be manipulated so as to lay the blame on him and thereby exonerate the lover boy. This doorman can be recognized as the infamous Koos Hertogs, a so-called serial killer, who is serving a long prison sentence in the Netherlands for the murder of young girls, a crime which according to Slobodan Mitric he did not commit. Something that other observers have suspected all along without being able to substantiate it.

Why The Hague Mouse remains unnamed in this book as a matter of precaution becomes obvious from what Mitric, who knew Koos Hertogs well, recently divulged: "Koos was a member of one of the most dangerous international terrorist gangs operating under the IDB (Dutch CIA). Their goal was to stage a couple of coups in Africa and to liquidate a Prime Minister. For this they had 100 heavy guys and 10 million U.S. dollars. WACE (World Atomic Contra Espionage) in cooperation with Dutch Counter Intelligence prevented this. But the Dutch government did not thank Dr. Troub-

lemaker [pseudonym for Mitric used in his book *The Golden Tip*]
for infiltrating into the heart of the gang - and for leading the entire
counter operation with among others [former Dutch resistance lead-
er] Hans Teengs Gerritsen. In order to hush things up, the Dutch
government accused Koos of child murder. When Dr. Troublemaker
protested, he was also accused of allegedly raping dozens of Dutch
prostitutes and wives of top criminals.

In his novel *Nederland's Mafia* [Netherlands Mafia, not trans-
lated] Dr. Troublemaker described 10 percent of all those foul corrupt practices of the Dutch government. Thus, the remaining 90
percent will be presented to the world in future books, provided Dr.
Troublemaker survives.

This case concerned more than 20 murders. Children were
ordered to be brought to wealthy and influential customers - some
were even ministers. If a girl threatened to talk, she was murdered.

If the whole truth will ever surface, I [Mitric] think that the
Netherlands will fall apart.

For occupying myself with this case in 1980-91 and making a
statement to the police in the Dutch province of Drenthe, I was
gagged. There followed a series of false testimonies that I supposedly would have raped dozens of prostitutes. All that was concocted
by Dutch officials in high places. A deal was then made with Koos
Hertogs. If he were to keep his mouth shut, he would be released
earlier. But Koos is only a small pawn in the whole game.

I have known him since 1974, when he was jailed for a minor
offense in the coastal town of Scheveningen near The Hague. Later,
I had many contacts with him. He visited me in prison and I also
met him often outside, because when I was imprisoned in Scheveningen (from 1975 to 1979), I was allowed to go out every day.
Koos told me everything in confidence before he was arrested. I told
a lawyer in confidence which important person it was, because I
believed that mankind could not tolerate such things. After all, they
were all innocent children abused by this dangerous pedophile gang
and then murdered. That lawyer advised me to keep my mouth shut.
Thanks to that, I was in 1977 nevertheless declared to be an undesirable alien, but until 1979 I could still go out every day. Only
when I told them that I was planning to write a novel about these
horrible things, was I transferred to the Mesdag Clinic [psychiatric
penitentiary] by Dutch royal body guards, who functioned as an
arrest team (read: liquidation team).

After promising that I would not mention that highest person in
my novels, I was released from Mesdag Clinic, but then again put in

solitary confinement in prison in Maastricht. And after the Secret Service (BVD) had promised me that everything would be okay, if I just promised to keep my mouth shut, I was taken by the BVD man Kuiper to a jail in Esserheem. There I got my car back and could go out whenever I wanted.

After Koos was arrested sometime in 1981 or 1982, I do not know exactly when, I testified to the police that he was innocent. But then a real witch hunt against me began. Dozens of police of the arrest team led by Arjo de Jong attacked me in jail with drawn weapons. Also they threatened to shoot me, if I were to mention that very important person. Even Attorney General Feber threatened me with death, if I would publish the truth. As I mentioned above, part of this whole affair is described in my novel *Netherlands' Mafia*...

The top person in charge of everything, I could not name. Who knows, maybe *Nederland's Mafia 2* will still come out.

Then there is [Dutch crime reporter and television producer] Peter R. de Vries. He is a friend of those influential people, who have also given him a great deal of money; his purpose is to shove all the blame onto Koos Hertogs. Koos is no darling. He is a very vulgar and slick security service man, and in many ways worse than any real criminal. But he has served enough time in jail for his part in this whole sordid affair.

I think that they now want to make him disappear forever from this world. Especially since the mafia has been blackmailing the top personality in this affair for years and they do not need Koos Hertogs anymore. This would be a pity, because Koos knows a lot and with a fair trial he would at least be of service to humanity, if he could testify. Koos also knows the top personality in the plutonium case (see the appendix – *Karate Bob and Prime Minister Lubbers' Muslim Bomb*).

Koos mediated between the Dutch top civil servant planning to liquidate a president in Africa and me, - of course they did not know that I was already working with Reserve Police International; they thought I was a liquidation agent.

You Dutch should really be ashamed of yourselves; all the trash in this world in the last thirty years comes from your corrupt secret services.

 Regarding [the deceased judge] Mr. Stolk, he is not been such an important person in the child murders. It is someone else with much more power, and this person is still alive!"

The last reference is obviously to The Hague Mouse.

Appendix II – The Lockerbie Disaster

This appendix contains documented material from *The Serbian Army* Nr. 3 – September 21, 1991 and is relevant to Chapter 3 dealing with the Lockerbie disaster "Aircraft Fall from the Sky Like Raindrops." These pages and more were contained as attachments to an article written by the publisher of this book entitled "Democracy on Trial" on the trials and tribulations of Slobodan Mitric. See appendix 3 for the first page of the article and other attachments; for the whole article: http://willehalminstitute.blogspot.com

THE UNITED STATES OF AMERICA AMERIC
CONSULATE
OFFICIAL BUSINESS FRANKFURT
GERMAN

U.S. DEPARTMENT OF JUSTICE
Immigration & Naturalization Service ESUCHT
c/o American Consulate General
11 Siesmayerstrasse
6000 Frankfurt/Main, Germany

1. dokazni materijal pronadjen kod
pripadnika FBI u amsterdamu koji su
krivi za avijonsku katastrofu Bojinga
747 koji je eksplodirao iznad Škotske.
... cela ova grupa FBI je umešana u
internacijonalno krijumčarenje droga..

1. Evidence found in the possession of members of the FBI in Amsterdam, who are guilty of the Lockerbie disaster with the Boeing 747, which exploded above Lockerbie... This whole FBI group is involved in the international drug trade...

2. dokument koji je potpisao direktor
PANAM agencije u Amsterdamu kad je
primijo brošuru šematskog prikaza
BOINGA 747 koji je eksplodirao iznad
Škotske... posle toga cela agencija
PANAMA je zatvorena????????????????????

2. Document that was signed by the Pan Am director in Amsterdam as a receipt for the booklet of the Training Program Development of the Boeing 747 that exploded above Scotland... Afterwards the whole Pan Am office was closed??????????????????????

3.Na ovom brodu spavali su pripadnici
FBI koji su krijumčarili drogu i koji
su umešani u mnoge terorističke akcije
obaranja USA avijona....da bi skinali
sumnju sa sebe bili su primorani da
se uhvati nekoliko hiljada kg. kokaji-
ne u Francuskoj/posle pada avijona
Boing 747 iznad Škotske....

3. In this boat slept members of the FBI, who were smuggling drugs and who were involved in many terrorist actions to down US aircraft... In order to divert the suspicion of their involvement in de crash of the Boeing 747 above Scotland, they were forced to catch a couple of thousand kilo's cocaine in France...

Note from the publisher. This is the boat mentioned at the end of chapter 3 "Airplanes Fall From the Sky Like Raindrops" in which the "FBI lawyer" waiting for the terrorists that parachuted out of the Boeing that would a little later explode above Lockerbie.

Appendix III – *Democracy on Trial*

This is page 1 of the article published in *The Serbian Army* Nr. 5, March 21, 1992 after it was, as the note below reads, refused for publication by the weekly *Observer* in England. The subtitle reads: "Former Secret Agent of Tito and *Enfant Terrible* of the Intelligence Services Slobodan Mitric, alias Karate Bob, accuses his accusers of foul play and corruption and suspects US President Bush and DEA boss William Bennett of covering up the Lockerbie affair." See the next two pages for related documents from *The Serbian Army* Nr. 4, Dec. 21 1991.

CPПCKA APMИJA — THE SERBIAN ARMY — L'ARMÉE SERBE

Note: The following article "Democracy on Trial" is a slightly revised version of a documented report that was sent for publication to the Editor-in-Chief of the English weekly newspaper "The Observer" in London on 21 February. Until this point of writing (8 March), no reply has been received. This report was based on various pamphlets and books written by Slobodan R. Mitric, conversations with him, and a study of all the evidence and material concerning his latest courtcase which was supplied to me through the courtesy of his present lawyer Mr Korvinus in Amsterdam. It was written before it was brought to my attention that on 18 February Mr Mitric had been appointed Defense Minister of the Free State of Serbia and in this capacity on 3 March, the day of his marriage to Iris de Vries, had issued an urgent call to the Secretary of the UN, Mr Boetros Ghali, not to send UN troops to the territory of Free Serbia...(RJK)

DEMOCRACY ON TRIAL

BY ROBERT J. KELDER

Former Secret Agent of Tito and Enfant Terrible of the Intelligence Services Slobodan Mitric, alias Karate Bob, accuses his accusers in Holland of foul play and corruption and suspects US President Bush and DEA boss William Bennett of covering up the truth behind the Lockerbie affair.

22

93

TERRORISM

THE SERBIAN ARMY IN WAR AGAINST DRUGS AND TERRORISM

BY:GEN. BRANISLAV HARAMBAŠIĆ

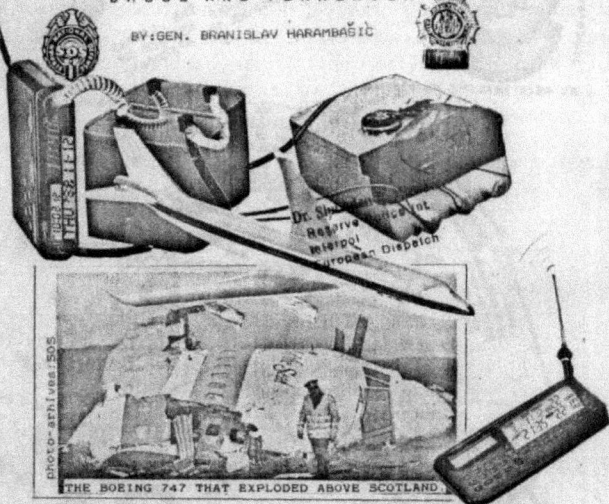

THE BOEING 747 THAT EXPLODED ABOVE SCOTLAND

ONE SHOULD NOT PLAY WITH HUMAN LIFES... AND ONE SHOULD NOT PLAY WITH THE DEAD... THE DEAD CRY OUT, THAT THIS MURDER OUTRAGE MUST BE JUGED. MISTER BUSH AND MISTER BENNETT, WAS IT NOT A FACT THAT YOU DID WANT TO HIDE THE TRUTH... NOBODY HATES MOSLEM MORE THAN I DO / BUT TO SPREAD LIES AND TO INSULT INNOCENT PEOPLE / THAT IS LIKE SPITTING STRAIGHT IN GOD'S FACE / DID YOU FORGET THAT MISTER GEORGE BUSH? IT IS THE DRUGSMAFFIA WHO DID LET EXPLODE THIS AND OTHER AIRPLANES / YOU KNOW THAT,MISTER BENNETT/ AND YOU KNOW THAT TOO,MISTER BUSH. IF YOU DO NOT KNOW THAT,THEN YOU SHOULD GIVE THE CHAIR YOU SIT UPON,TO ANOTHER PERSON...AS YOU SHOULD KNOW WHO YOU HAVE AMIDST YOURSELVES IN THE; F.B.I/D.E.A./C.I.A. AND YOU SHOULD ALSO KNOW THE NAMES OF THE TWO SENATORS WHO DO HELP THE DRUGSMAFFIA IN EXCHANGE FOR THE DOLLARS THAT DID HELP YOU TO WIN THE ELECTIONS. AND IT IS UP TO YOU ,MISTER PRESIDENT ,TO RIGHTEOUSLY SOLVE THIS, OUT OF RESPECT FOR THE DEAD,GOD DEMANDS THAT OF YOU...

153

The introduction to the article "Democracy on Trial" started by quoting the passage from the above page from *The Serbian Army* Nr. 4 and continued as follows: "It is these and other grave charges such as the complicity of Dutch Prime Minister Lubbers in atomic espionage and the theft of plutonium that are to be found together with photos and documentary material in the most recent issues of the quarterly trilingual (Serbian, English and French) magazine *The Serbian Army* published by Dr. Slobodan Mitric in Amsterdam.

These startling allegations on the dubious roles played by the high and mighty of this world in protecting their own selfish interests form only the tip of the iceberg. They do not only seriously question that no one stands above the law, but also cast great doubt on the observance of the very principle on which democratic government is founded, namely the system of checks and balances between the legislative, executive and judicial powers.

If further investigated and found to be true, they would no doubt cause a major political upheaval. Part and parcel of the alarming accusations made by Mitric and his associates is furthermore that the long arm of the law and the tentacles of the mafia are, as it were, often walking hand in hand. It is therefore not surprising that until now no court of law in The Netherlands has provided Mitric with any real opportunity to air his grievances and substantiate his charges and that he has been sentenced for crimes, he says he did not commit. [Something that I as a witness in his last court case can personally corroborate].

But who in heaven's name is this man issuing these hard-hitting charges? What has he in turn been charged with? And is the fact that other inside information supplied by him in the past has been borne out by the course of succeeding events an indication that his latest salvo is not merely a shot in the dark?"

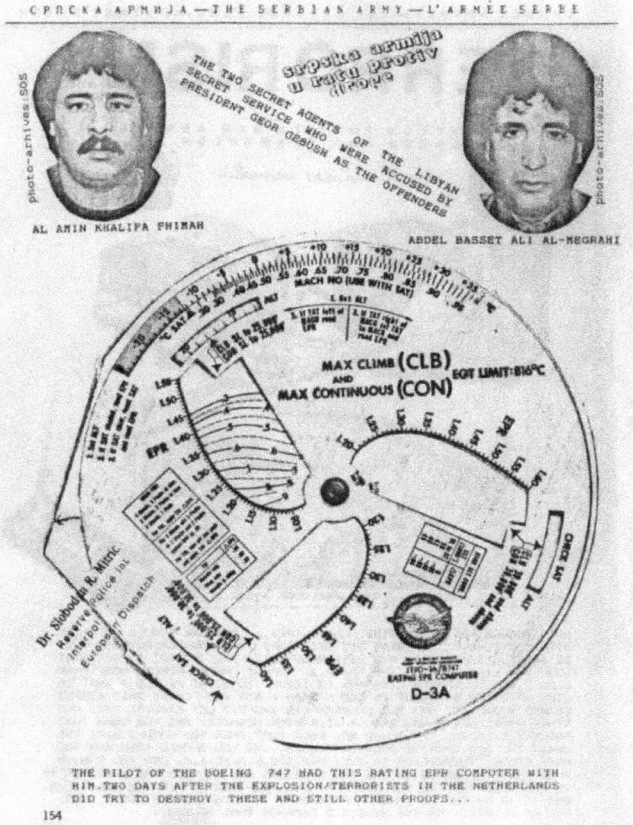

CPRCKA APMHJA —THE SERBIAN ARMY—L'ARMÉE SERBE

photo-arhives-SOS

THE TWO SECRET AGENTS OF THE SECRET SERVICE WHO WERE ACCUSED BY PRESIDENT GEOR GEBUSH AS THE LIBYAN OFFENDERS

srpska armija u fraru protiv Evrope

photo-arhives-SOS

AL AMIN KHALIFA FHIMAH

ABDEL BASSET ALI AL-MEGRAHI

MAX CLIMB (CLB) AND MAX CONTINUOUS (CON) EGT LIMIT:816°C

Dr. Slobodan R. Mitric Reserve police int. Interpol Dispatch European Dispatch

D-3A

THE PILOT OF THE BOEING 747 HAD THIS RATING EPR COMPUTER WITH HIM. TWO DAYS AFTER THE EXPLOSION/TERRORISTS IN THE NETHERLANDS DID TRY TO DESTROY THESE AND STILL OTHER PROOFS...

154

95

the serbian army in war against drugs

"PRESIDENT GEORGE BUSH IN THE TIMES, THAT HE WAS THE BOSS OF THE C.I.A."

THE BOSS OF DEA WILLIAM BENNETT/ HE SHOULD KNOW WHO THE REAL OFFENDERS ARE

THE SAME RATING EPR COMPUTER SEEN FROM THE OTHER SIDE...

155

William Bennett as a top official (contractor) of the CIA and also his colleague Bush were apparently not only aware of the background to the Lockerbie disaster, but also knew well in advance that 9/11 was being planned, as the author charges in his letter to his readers and the people of the world on the back flap of this book. This is borne out by the next two appendices.

96

Appendix IV – On the Murder of Bill Bennett

Letter by Slobodan Mitric to an Editor of the Dutch Newspaper *TROUW* on the Murder of Former CIA Contractor Bill Bennett

Dear ...,

Today, April 20, 2009, is Serbian Easter. And I have a journalistic gift for you.

On March 22 last in the U.S., Bill Bennett was murdered.

Bill was one of the CIA men, who in the eighties was given documents about terrorist plans to attack vital targets in the U.S.: Twin Towers in New York, the Senate, the White House, the Pentagon in Washington, a nuclear power plant in the U.S. etc...

Bill his wife Cindy were walking when he was killed by a number of masked men with sticks which they used to beat him to death.

It is unofficially known that Bill was responsible for the attack by "mistake" by U.S. aircrafts on the Chinese embassy in Belgrade. Through this "failure", 20 other CIA people were fired from the CIA in 2000.

Bill was directly involved in that bombing by giving the U.S. Air Force the plans to bomb that target and then maintaining that the wrong target was bombed ...

Baloney of course. Bill gave his top spy in Belgrade with the code name "Tsar" (now also murdered) a miniature transmitter to plant in a military complex in New Belgrade. "Tsar" was a KGB / CIA double agent with good connections as well to the IDB [Dutch Foreign Intelligence] in The Hague. "Tsar" deliberately placed that miniature transmitter not in the military complex, as was meant, but in the Chinese Embassy ... This discredited the U.S. and only at the last minute it could be prevented that through this failure the conflict was widened.

Anyway, Bennett was liquidated, because according to the perpetrators evidence concerning the terrorist attacks on the Twin Towers must at all costs be suppressed.

I hope you can undertake further investigative journalism for TROUW [Dutch national, Christian orientated newspaper in Amsterdam, founded by the resistance during WWII], or are your hands and feet tied there?

It is not an everyday news item that a CIA man was killed in the U.S. and on top of that such an important person.

Whose turn is it now...?

Except Bill Bennett also former President Bush and Bill Webster (former FBI director, who later became CIA director) knew exactly when and by whom the terrorist attacks on U.S. targets with aircraft were going to be carried out.

Regards,
Slobodan Slobodan

Note by the publisher: Nothing was apparently done with this letter.

97

Appendix V – Letter to Phil

Letter published in *The Serbian Army* by Milorad G. Markovich, Mitric's CIA connection, to US Senator Phil Crane on Mitric's Discovery of a Training Camp in Amsterdam of an International Ring of Terrorists

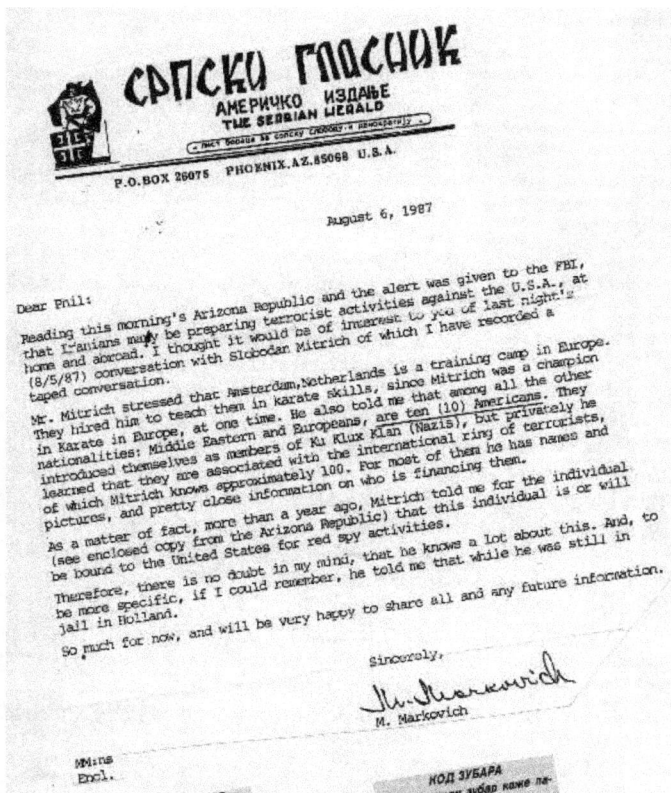

СРПСКИ ГЛАСНИК
АМЕРИЧКО ИЗДАЊЕ
THE SERBIAN HERALD

P.O.BOX 26075   PHOENIX,AZ,85068 U.S.A.

August 6, 1987

Dear Phil:

Reading this morning's Arizona Republic and the alert was given to the FBI, that Iranians may be preparing terrorist activities against the U.S.A., at home and abroad. I thought it would be of interest to you of last night's (8/5/87) conversation with Slobodan Mitrich of which I have recorded a taped conversation.

Mr. Mitrich stressed that Amsterdam,Netherlands is a training camp in Europe. They hired him to teach them in karate skills, since Mitrich was a champion in Karate in Europe, at one time. He also told me that among all the other nationalities: Middle Eastern and Europeans, are ten (10) Americans. They introduced themselves as members of Ku Klux Klan (Nazis), but privately he learned that they are associated with the international ring of terrorists, of which Mitrich knows approximately 100. For most of them he has names and pictures, and pretty close information on who is financing them.

As a matter of fact, more than a year ago, Mitrich told me for the individual (see enclosed copy from the Arizona Republic) that this individual is or will be bound to the United States for red spy activities.

Therefore, there is no doubt in my mind, that he knows a lot about this. And, to be more specific, if I could remember, he told me that while he was still in jail in Holland.

So much for now, and will be very happy to share all and any future information.

Sincerely,

M. Markovich

MM:ns
Encl.

КОД ЗУБАРА
...ни зубар каже па-

98

Appendix VI – Ustasha in Texel

Ustasha Train for Parachute Jumping and
Other Terrorist Related Actions in The Netherlands

The following 4 pages contain 2 articles relevant to chapter 4 "TEXEL".

СРПСКА АРМИЈА БР.8. 21 ДЕЦЕМБАР 1992 СТРАНА 41
РОН ВАН ДАРТЕЛ - АМБАСАДОР ХОЛАНДИЈЕ
ХОЛАНДСКИ ШПИЈУН У БЕОГРАДУ
- ПОБРАТИМ бориса грозног -
ОБА ТРАЖЕ ГЛАВУ СЛОБОДАНА ПИВЉАНИНА

USTAŠE TRENIRAJU PADOBRANSTVO I OSTALE
TERORISTIČKE AKCIJE U NIZOZEMSKOJ, I TO U
VREME KAD HASAN VAN DEN BROEK, MINISTAR
INISTRANIH POSLOVA OVE DO NEDAVNO
GOSTOLJUBIVE DRŽAVE PRETI BOMBARDOVANJEM
BEOGRADA I OSTALIH SRPSKIH TERITORIJA.
SVE SE OVO ODVIJA NARAVNO UZ SAGLASNOST
NIZOZEMSKIH TAJNIH SLUŽBI.NA OSTRVU
TAXELU A I U DRUGIM VOJNIM BAZAMA,ŠIROM
NIZOZEMSKE, TRENIRAJU SE USTAŠKI
BOJOVNICI, MUSLIMANSKE ZELENE BARETE I
ŠIPTARI SA KOSOVA KOJI ĆE,NAKON USPEŠNE
OBUKE DA SKAČU U NAŠE SRPSKE KRAJEVE I DA
KOLJU SRPSKU NEJAČ...
OVE RAZBOJNIKE TRENIRA LIČNI PRIJATELJ
PRESJEDNIKA NIZOZEMSKE RUDA LUBERSA,
PUKOVNIK VAN NOORT .
OVO NIJE JEDINA GRUPA KOJA SE OVDE OBUČAVA... PRE IZBIJANJA ORUŽANIH SUKOBA NA
TERITORIJAMA BIVŠE JUGOSLAVIJE U NIZOZEMSKOJ SU SE OBUČAVALI INTERNACIONALNI
KRIJUMČARI DROGE KOJI BI POSLE USPELOG TRENINGA SKAKANJA PADOBRANOM ONDA ZA NIZOZEMSKU
MAFIJU (KOJOM INAČE VODE NAJUGLEDNIJI HOLANDSKI GLUMCI, PISCI, POLICIJSKI
SLUŽBENICI,PRAVNICI, POLITIČARI ITD...) SNAKLI SA PADOBRANOM I U RUSAKU NOSILI PO
DESETAK KILIGRAMA HEROJINA ILI KOKAJINA,...
MEDJU TIM NIZOZEMSKIM SAVEZNICIMA BILO JE UVEK MNOGO HRVATA /MUSLIMANA I ŠIPTARA...
JAVNA JE TAJANA DA SU NIZOZEMSKI KRIMINALCI LIKVIDIRALI PRESJEDNIKA ŠVETSKE ULOPA
PALMEA,A OD NEDAVNO ŠAPUČE SE DA SU JELCINJA DROGIRALI U HOTELU HILTONU U AMSTERDAMU U
VREME NJEGOVE POSETE HOLANDIJI STAVIVŠI MU KOKAJIN U PIĆE PA KAD JE BIJO U TRANSU SA
JELSINOM SKLOPILI UGOVOR DA MU POMOGNU DA DODJE NA VLAST GDE SU UBILI DESETAK
GRANICARA U LITONIJI/PA SAD ŠANTIRAJU JELSINJA I NJEGOVU KLIKU ...
SVET JOŠ NIJE UVIDEO DA SU: NAJVEĆI ORGANIZATORI I TRGOVACI DROGOM, ORUŽJEM,BELIM
ROBLJEM U STVARI NIZOZEMCI,GDE U POSLEDNJE VREME VRŠE I ATENTATE ...

Ustasha Train for Parachute Jumping

The Serbian Army, Nr. 8 - December 21 1992, P. 41

Ustasha [Croatian fascists] train for parachute jumping and other terrorist related actions in the Netherlands. And please note, at the same time that Mr. Hasan [Hans] van den Broek, Minister of Foreign Affairs of this previously so hospitable state, threatens to bomb Belgrade and other Serbian territories. All this occurs, of course, with permission from various Dutch secret services.

On the island of Texel, as in other other military bases in the Netherlands, Ustasha murder commandos, Muslim Green Berets and Schiptars [Albanians from Kosovo] are being trained, who after successfully completing their training will jump on our Serbian territories and kill innocent Serbian civilians.

These bandits receive their training from Colonel Van Noort, a personal friend of Dutch Prime Minister Ruud Lubbers.

This is not the only group that is being trained. Before the outbreak of armed conflicts on the territories of the former Yugoslavia, international smugglers of drugs were trained in the Netherlands for sky diving. Upon completing their training they often parachuted with tens of kilo's heroin in their back packs – in this case for the Dutch Mafia (which was as a matter of fact led by the most eminent film actors, writers, police officers, lawyers, politicians etc.) Among these Dutch allies were always many Croats, Muslims (from Bosnia) and Albanians (from Kosovo).

It is a public secret that Dutch criminals liquidated the Prime Minister of Sweden, Olof Palme. And recently, it was whispered that [the Russian politician] Yeltsin had been drugged in Hotel Hilton in Amsterdam during the time that he visited the Netherlands. Cocaine was mixed in his drink and when he was in a trance, an agreement was made to help him get to power, after which 10 border guards were murdered in Lithuania. Now Yeltsin and his clique are being blackmailed.

The world does not yet realize that the biggest organizers and dealers in drugs, weapons, white slavery (trade in women) are in fact the Dutch, who recently are also carrying out assassinations.

"War Criminal Of The Kingdom Of The Netherlands"

The Serbian Army, Nr. 11 - September 1993

Caption to the left - Ron van Dartel - Ambassador of the Netherlands (Dutch spy in Belgrade), Brother of Boris the Terrible [Boris Tadic] - both looking for the head of Slobodan Pivljanina [Mitric].

Text in the middle - Colonel Wil van Noort receiving an award from [Croatian President] Franco Tudjman
Dutch Colonel Wil van Noort, a great friend of Prime Minister Lubbers of the Netherlands, Ruda (read thieves), argues that the Netherlands should recognize the borders of Croatia that Hitler recognized. It is interesting to note that the father of Lubbers was one of the leading resistance fighters during the Second World War against the Germans; all this hatred against the Serbs - the people who side by side with his father fought against Dutch and Croatian Nazis – on the part of the Prime Minster is therefore incomprehensible.

Chart 3 below – The independent state of Croatia during Hitler – behind its realization stands Colonel van Noort.

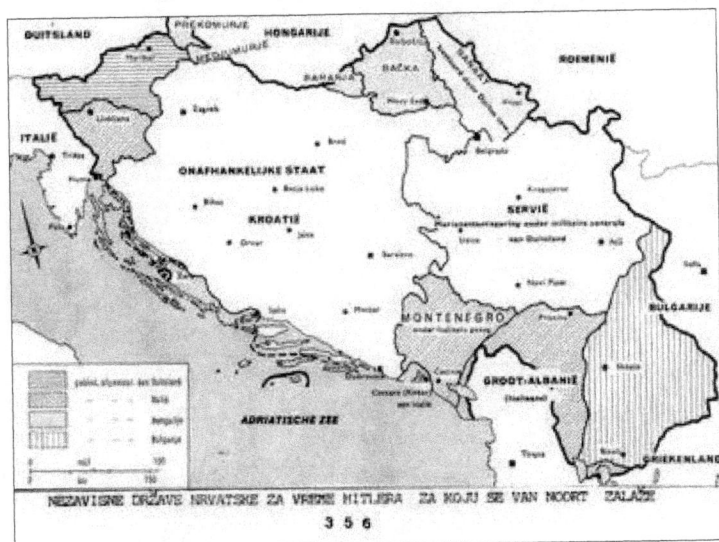

NEZAVISNE DRŽAVE NRVATSKE ZA VRIME HITLJERA ZA KOJU SE VAN NOORT ZALAZE

3 5 6

Appendix VII – The 9/11 Forewarnings

The following pages contain some of the photos from the pages of *The Serbian Army*, beginning with the planned attack on the Senate, that were shown well in advance of 9/11 during the first secret joint American-Russian anti-terrorism conference as described in Chapter 7 "I am that terrorist!" and that were as forewarnings of 9/11 also sent to, among others, all heads of leading states and directors of intelligence agencies. The "terrorist" Nick in the foreground of all these images is the adjunct-director of World Atomic Counter-espionage (WACE. Also the links are provided to the corresponding issues of *The Serbian Army*.

The Serbian Army, Nr. 9 – March 21, 1993

https://acrobat.com/#d=mhgbqfJLQEGZqUnh-p32-Q

Planned Attack on the Twin Towers from Above and Below

The Serbian Army, Nr. 8 – December 21, 1992

Planned Attack on the United Nations from Above and Below

The Serbian Army, Nr. 10 – June 21, 1993, p. 41

https://acrobat.com/#d=1EMkVkq6Qdq*hVGRH0KBDQ

Planned Attack on the Parliament in The Hague, Netherlands

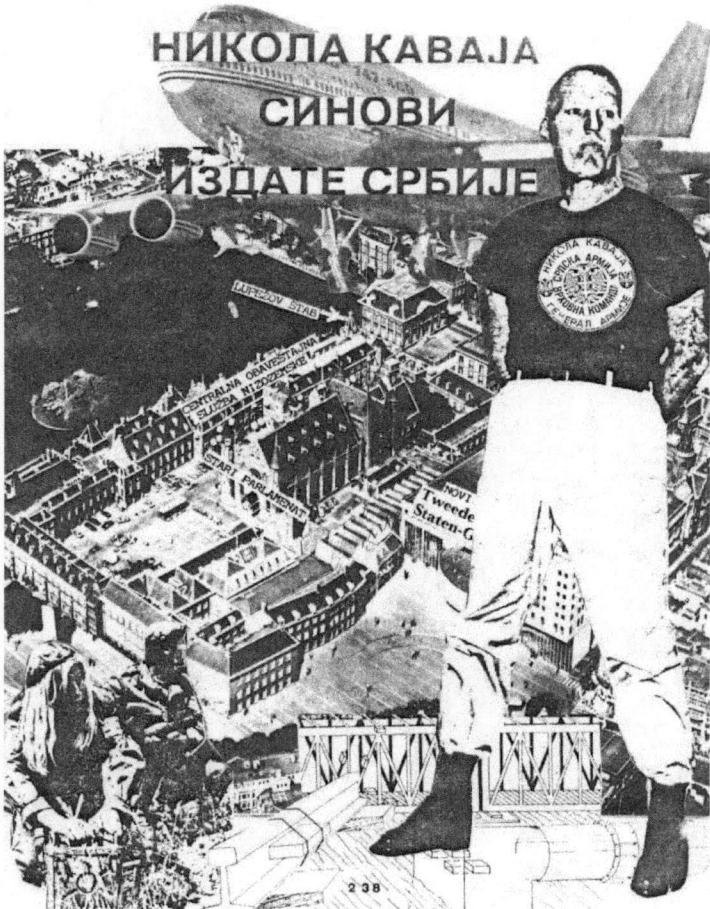

The Serbian Army Nr. 11 – September 21, 1993, p. 238

https://acrobat.com/#d=e8B4NUNGQh*c5yvqwsC4tA

Planned Attack on the Central Bank in Frankfurt, Germany

The Serbian Army **Nr. 12, December 21 1993, p. 254**

https://acrobat.com/#d=1EMkVkq6Qdq*hVGRH0KBDQ

Appendix VIII – *Operation Twins* 1993

The first time that excerpts from *Operation Twins I* were published in the open was with this title page in *The Serbian Army* - Nr. 12, December 21 1993 p. 702 -718. The second page with the author's foreword is shown on the next page, which also includes the name of the publisher *The Serbian Lions* in Amsterdam that pre-published the whole trilogy in Serbian and English for internal use and the date of publication 1982.

At the end of this excerpt, the editor wrote the following epilogue, "In this issue of *The Serbian Army*, we have published a few chapters from *Operation Twins*. This book consists of three volumes, totaling 700 pages, including 36 appendices. However, until this present day, this book has not been published, because it was confiscated by the CIA (as was the case with many books by Slobodan Mitric: *The Underworld of Belgrade* was confiscated by the Yugoslav Secret Service, UDBA in 1971; *The Swedish Mafia* by the Swedish Secret Service SEPO in 1973; *The Murder Machine of Belgrade* by the BVD [Dutch version of the FBI]; his Dutch books *Tito's Murder Machine* and *Tito's Secret Agent* were taken off the shelves and *Netherlands' Mafia* was forbidden by the Dutch Ministry of Justice.)

The CIA was able to get the book in question that they then confiscated through the work of their secret agents Mike Djordjevic (code name Boyer) and Dr. Milorad G. Markovic (code name 0008+). However, we succeeded in getting a copy of the first volume that was stored in a safe place." (see: https://acrobat.com/#d=wVOjjEuHX6cdByBwXuaMaQ)

Second page of the Excerpts from
Operation Twins I with a Foreword by the Author

This book is a product of the imagination
Carved out by pure truth
On the edge of confession
Of a man's consciousness…
If anyone recognizes himself,
It is pure coincidence
And if a character from this book exists today,
At this moment
With a slightly different identity,
But real personality,
That is pure coincidence too.

A lapse of memory,
A mistake of the unconscious.
The streets, towns, and states might be true,
But they merely hide the pure spirit of the book:
Pure fantasy,
A description of the world of the future
We are walking through today,
A work of fiction,
A lie,
Written by a man's hand,
Since we know no other way.
Written about the future,
We have already forgotten the past.
The present we are ashamed of.
Hidden in our asilum ignorantia
Our entelecheia breaks the cage
Carrying the torch of history
To other galaxies:
Of the past,
Of the present,
Of the future.
The one reading this book without disbelief
Is its biggest friend,
And there is a kernel of hope in his soul.

Slobodan Radojev Mitric
December 24, 1982

Appendix IX – *Operation Twins:* The Screen-play

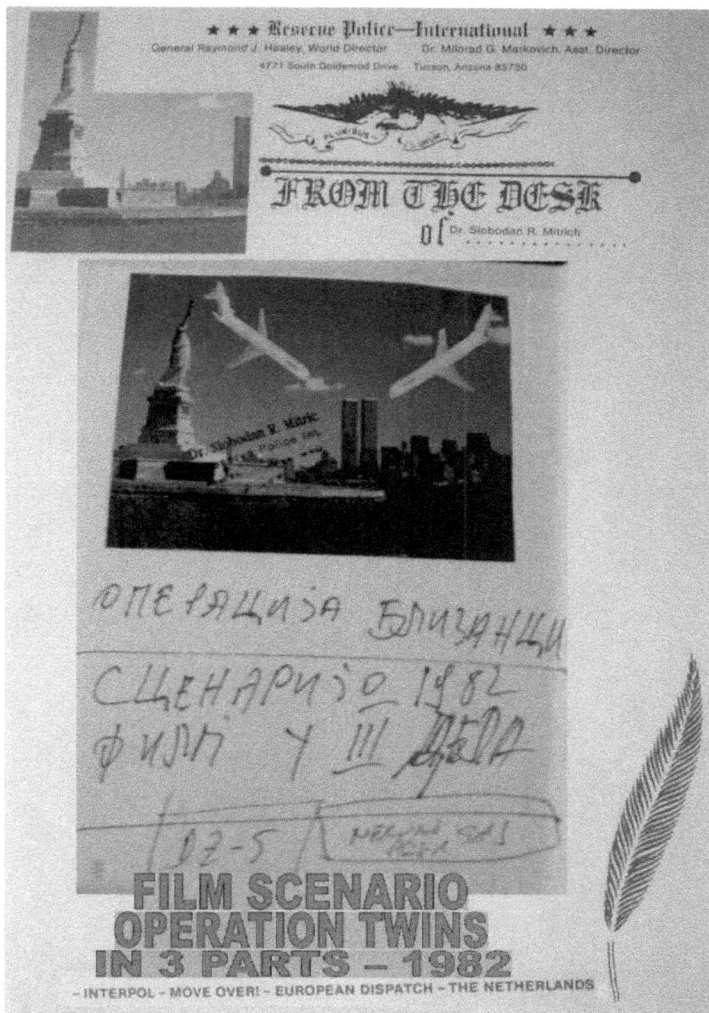

Title page of the screen-play with the letterhead used since 1986 by of the European RPI Desk of Dr. Slobodan Mitric. This feature film project had an impressive line-up of actors and actresses such as Burt Lancaster, Paul Newman and Sophia Loren and even enjoyed the backing of President Reagan, but was abandoned when the CIA confiscated the manuscript.

Appendix X – *ОПЕРАЦИЈА БЛИЗАНЦИ*

Title Page of the Serbian Edition of *Operation Twins* I

СЛОБОДАН РАДОЈЕВ МИТРИЋ

ОПЕРАЦИЈА БЛИЗАНЦИ

Published by the Author, Slobodan Radojev Mitric in 1999
in Amsterdam in his L'Atelier de la Liberté/
Laboratory of Freedom (ISBN 90-803811-3-6)

"Ronnie has personally admitted to me that after reading this manuscript [*Operation Twins*], he decided to negotiate with Moscow (...) about nuclear disarmament and the mutual struggle against terrorism," says General Raymond Healey, Director World Atomic Counter Espionage (WACE) to CIA Director William Casey in Chapter 53 of this book. And as former CIA Director for the Soviet Union, James Jesus Angleton, upon recognizing himself as one the main characters of *Operation Twins* said to his former close colleague Slobodan Mitric, "It is the absolute truth."

For the original Serbian version of this prophetic science fiction trilogy set in the last three days of the last millennium, the author in 1986 was awarded an honorary degree in law from a Police Academy in Arizona. A planned film version with the backing of President Reagan did not materialize; the CIA confiscated the manuscript. In the P.S. to his letter on the next page regarding CIA involvement in Sadam's so-called WMD's, the author writes, "The CIA was aware of all these plans in 1982 because they were able to lay their hands on *Operation Twins*. I am slowly beginning to wonder: were these agents who told me all that in detail also not sent to me by the CIA and MOSSAD in order to afterwards prepare their dirty wars, which are now already taking place? If I think things over well, I would not be surprised if that were indeed the case. Anyway, it is only in the United States and nowhere else that an answer to all these questions can be given."

Among the 21 appendices on the turbulent life and as yet unrecognized work of the writer is vital background and inside information on the author's frequent but unheeded forewarnings of 9 /11.

The retranslated version of part 1 of this trilogy was presented by the Willehalm Institute press on March 2005 in the national press center in The Hague, Netherlands next to the parliament buildings.

Operation Twins, Part 1 (ISBN 90-73932-05-X, 192 p.) can be ordered at the bookstore, www.BoekenRoute.nl or from the publisher by sending an email: info@willehalm.nl; www.willehalm.nl/operationtwins.htm

OPERATION TWINS

World War Three is set to begin at three minutes before midnight Eastern Standard Time, Dec. 31, 1999.

Thousands of intercontinental nuclear missiles are ready to be launched from Russia to strike the USA and the European Community...

Thousands of mini-atomic bombs, hidden in diplomatic suitcases, have been placed in the center of the main NATO security and defense buildings.

Thousands of specially trained Russian kamikazes, disguised as NATO soldiers, are taking over every important building of the North Atlantic Treaty Organization...

This decoded message from a top US spy in the Kremlin named 'Fedora' was delivered to the president of the United States of America in 1982.

World War Three is set to begin at three minutes before midnight Moscow Time, Dec. 31, 1999.

Thousands of intercontinental nuclear missiles are ready to be launched from the USA and the European Community to strike Russia...

Thousands of mini-atomic bombs hidden in backpacks have been placed in the center of the main Warsaw Pact security and defense buildings.

Thousands of specially trained NATO kamikazes, disguised as Warsaw Pact soldiers, are taking over every important building in the USSR ...

This decoded message from a top Soviet spy in the White House named 'Andrew' was delivered to the General Secretary of the USSR Communist Party in 1982.

Secretly written and translated into English at the height of the Cold War in 1982, this first volume of a trilogy by former Yugoslav Special Secret Service agent Slobodan R. Mitric (Karate Bob) describes the events, from the perspective of both East and West, leading up to World War III from Dec. 25 to Dec. 29, 1999. The next two volumes take place on Dec. 29 until the last three minutes of the past millennium. These two volumes were confiscated by the CIA in 1987 and full-fledged plans to turn this spy thriller into a movie with an international cast of stars and the backing of US President Ronald Reagan were abandoned.

After a futile attempt on the part of the author through the publisher in 1999 to get the complete trilogy published in the USA in order to prevent the 9/11 disaster, this initial volume *Operation Twins* has now finally been made available to the general public. The 21 appendices contain many hitherto unpublished documents that shed an amazing light on the author's remarkable course of life and his dramatic plight as Dutch, European and now World Director of *Reserve Police-International* to safeguard the planet from the imminent dangers of international (nuclear) terrorism.

ISBN 90-73932-05-X
© Willehalm Institute Press
www.willehalm.nl
Amsterdam, The Netherlands

<u>Appendix XIII – Letter by S. Mitric on Y2K and 9/11</u>

This letter refers, to my knowledge, to the most explicit and earliest advance warnings yet to the 9/11 disaster, dating as they do as far back as 1986. It was first published in English in *Operation Twins I*, after it had been sent and faxed to the recipient and other parties in the original Serbian.

K.O.S.A

Amsterdam, December 7, 2003

President of the Human Rights Association
Branislav Kujacic

Leka Vukalovic Street nr. 27
8901 Trebinje
Republic of Srpska

God bless you Bajo,
Thank you for your letter from 11-11-2003 and enclosures. I am glad that you [finally] wrote me after a long period [of silence]. How are you? Is someone writing to you from abroad? How is the situation there in brave Herzegovina and with its neighbors Monte-negro and Serbia? Please be so kind as to write and tell me all about it. Is it now better under Anglo-Saxon and Islamic occupation, or was it better under the yoke of Milosovic, slave in The Hague, or under the Marshall from Kumrovac*?

How are the farmers doing, the workers, scholars and students, pensioners and the sick? My health is very bad, I am quite sick, but my spirit is keeping me alive, and I hope it will stay like that until I can liberate our enslaved lands.

In your letter you ask me if I agree to your coming here to the Hague as a witness to testify about the hatred against the Serbs on the part of this [International] Justice Tribunal. You have my blessings. But are you invited by the Tribunal to be a witness? For if not, they will not let you testify. Submit a written request to be a witness and what you would like to testify about, and send that to that shameful anti-Serbian tribunal and demand that they reply.

Has the former commander of the Yugoslav army General Momcilo Perisic been invited to testify as a witness? What has happened to him after he was arrested and accused of spying? From your letter, I gather that you know him personally. If so, give him my greetings and tell him that I personally know Colonel Elmar Naber, from the period that he was a military attaché in the Hague (Colonel Elmar Naber, Lange Voorhout 102, Den Haag, tel. 070-6224911, local number of his office 370). Colonel Naber is a close friend of a general of Serbian descent named Slobodan Kovacevic, etc. etc. etc. If I could be of service to General Momcilo, tell him to contact me.

All the essential strands of information possessed by the American Intelligence Services regarding Serbs and Russians are in the hands of two double spies of so-called Serbian descent: Mike Djordjevic and Micirevic. I know both of them very well.
Djordjevic I met in Sweden in 1971. At that time, I disarmed a Yugoslav agent from Osijec named Rebrima Tomislav who had been ordered to execute me. All international and Yugoslavian newspapers reported this. After coming back from Yugoslavia, where I refused to work at the Intelligence and Counter-intelligence School in Zemun, Mr. Djordjevic together with a number of terrorists from Belgrade attacked me in downtown Stockholm. He insulted me, saying: "Chetnik motherfucker, are you the one who writes in this treacherous Chetnik newspaper of Marko Milunovic?"

Dear brother Bajo, I'll be short on all the horrible things with which this Skojevac insulted me. This resulted in my beating him up so severely that he was taken by an ambulance to the hospital, where he stayed for a couple of days.

In 1973, the commander of the Counter-Intelligence Service in Novisad Mr. Rados Nedic mentioned this case, accusing me of being a class enemy, because I had beaten up his best agent in the West.

In the middle of the eighties, I was cooperating with General Naber [in The Hague], a number of American generals and Serbs also had contact with me.

Mr. Milorad Markovic spoke many times about a certain Serb working for the CIA who supposedly wanted to help me come to America. I tried to discover the name of this man, but he did not dare give it to me. "No!" he said, "I've been forbidden to do this! I can't! He knows you personally and when you come over here, you'll understand everything," etc. etc. etc.

I got sick of all this conspiracy and told Mr. Markovic that he [this man] is not honest, for he is keeping his identity secret. "No, for this is how the CIA works!" Dr. Markovic said excusing himself. "Nonsense," I replied, "this man is hiding something." After that, Mr. Markovic when drunk, once told me over the telephone that that man was called Djordjevic. Shortly afterwards Mr. Markovic disappeared from this world.

The deceased Dr. Markovich was very well informed about America's top secrets. Among these, he told me confidentially already in 1986 that the son of George Bush would become America's president at the end of the last century and the beginning of the new millennium. Dr. Markovic told me [furthermore] that Slobodan Milosevic was preparing to come to power in Yugoslavia with the aid of some 3000 CIA agents. He asked me to join them, but I refused (Dr. Markovic is a niece of Mira Markovic-Milosevic). He [also] told me that America would bomb Belgrade, that Europe would restore the Roman Empire, and spoke about NATO plans to destroy Russia at the beginning of this millennium etc. etc. etc…

At the time that I was publishing *The Serbian Army,* I put out a number of photographs and articles about Mister-Comrade Djordjevic under the title "Is Mike Djordjevic a Member of UDBA or is Slobodan Milosevic a Member of the CIA?" (In reality, both were members of the UDBA as well as the CIA – according to the motto, who pays more. This is something of which I am convinced that history will prove me right).

Through my connections, I learned that Mike Djordjevic had told the American Government that I am supposed to be a hard-line Communist; since then they have made my life miserable.

This same non human-being wrote to Yugoslav communists claiming that I am a radical advocate of Great Serbia; after which Yugoslav Secret Service agents tried to execute me in September 1973 and again later at the end of December in Amsterdam, because I had refused to liquidate Vlado Dapcevich. This same non-person also said that I am a hard-line communist, Russian spy, Serbian nationalist and God knows what else, although I only met him twice in my life.

The first time was when I beat him up severely and the second time on February 1, 1972 in the Mariatorget subway station in Stockholm, where he apologized for having accused and insulted me, and where I apologized for beating him up. He was in the company of a big Russian man wearing a Russian fur hat. (I recognized this Russian from a meeting in the fall of 1971 in Banjica in the company of my SDB boss Obrad Grkovic and our SDB chauffeur a couple of hours before we got permission to enter the center of the Intelligence and Counter-Intelligence College that was housed in a military base at the Car Dusan street in Zemun). That day I had an appointment with members of the Swedish Secret Service in connection with the fight against drugs trafficking and international terrorism. I was negotiating a couple of months about working together with the Swedish Secret Service. They suggested I come with them to Poland, which I refused. I agreed [however] to cooperate with them in Scandinavia only in the fight against international terrorism and drugs. At that meeting was present, among others, the Commissioner of the Swedish Police, Mr. Sturenson, a member of the Finnish Secret Service Mr. Leif, a general of the British Secret Service MI5 and a Swedish woman, who was a member of the Swedish Intelligence Service IB. Until the present day, I do not know how Mr. Djordjevic found out about this meeting, but he was there and that is the reason for the distrust shown by the above-mentioned group of spies.

This group of agents warned me that in front of the secret apartment of the Swedish Secret Service SEPO where this meeting was taking place, there was a girl in the car parked in front of that apartment, who wanted to falsely accuse me of rape. Mr. Leif said that this was the work of Mr. Djordjevic and that Russian general. I had to laugh, thinking that they were joking. A day after this meeting, I was arrested and falsely charged with raping a couple of Swedish women. It is known to me that this non-person Djordjevic during his so-called desertion from the UDBA to the CIA confessed that he was an UDBA agent, but [if so] why did he remain silent about the above-mentioned facts? The Russian man with the big fur cap was [indeed] a general whose task it was to work on special operations for Tito's Secret Service Y.O.C.A, the Yugoslav Central Intelligence Agency.

Micirevic, also known as Rick Micir, I met in the underground nuclear bunker of the American Embassy in The Hague in the presence of the head of the Secret Service of the USA, Mr. Joe and a Dutch police commissioner, who was at that time working for Interpol. Micirevic is an inhuman bastard, who (supposedly) discovered that Saddam Hussein possesses an atom bomb. Micirevic together with that bully Bremer found out that after Saddam has eaten brown beans, he lets out unbearable farts. Both of them concluded that that these gases are dangerous biological weapons and that this must be the case, (the CIA after all knows everything) because he has, please excuse me for saying this, produced an atom bomb in his ass… and that [accordingly] Iraq must be bombed to pieces.
Dutch double agents from the IDB [the Dutch equivalent of the CIA] gave me a secret list of 100 American citizens with their addresses and every possible information on how they were fabricating biological weapons. A copy of this secret booklet was through me [i.e. through my services] given to, among others, Zlatan Stamenic in Washington.

Mr. Bremer, at that time US ambassador in The Hague, received this terrorist brochure from the head of security at the embassy, Mr. Brizinski. (Brizinski, an American with a Polish-Jewish background denied in the presence of my wife and two lawyers of mine that he ever received anything from me – prove it if you can, he told me brutally in 1986.) Bremer immediately went off to Washington with this brochure, where he became head of the anti-terrorist units. (At the request of General Healey and Zlatan Stamenic, I personally delivered this brochure and the secret list of 100 American citizens, who were making biological weapons and preparing actions on US territory, to the head of security at the American Embassy in The Hague in 1981 in the presence of one of the directors of the Dutch [National] Secret Service BVD Abel Kuiper. One of the people who helped get hold of this dangerous secret booklet, Vladimir Guljanin was extradited by the Dutch Foreign Secret Service IDB to Tito's Yugoslavia, where Tito had him executed immediately.) I openly told the Americans by telephone in the middle of the eighties that Bremer was a fag (pedophile in this case does not mean a homosexual, but a monstrous bully). Naturally, this fag has not forgiven me. In that period, I finished my book *Operation Twins*! The second and third volumes were confiscated by American-Russian double agents.

From 1986, onwards I was informed about the attacks by airplanes on the Twin Towers in New York – and also on the Pentagon, House of Congress and the White House in Washington.
All this was planned to happen on December 31, 1999 at 00.00 hours [midnight].
The truth of the matter is that [because of this] the USA forbade all flights for 24 hours on that very same day.
But it is also true that after the USA was informed about this beforehand, that Operation Twins was postponed (a special envoy of the CIA had taken the secret message and personally handed it over to the directors of the CIA, FBI and DIA and also a copy to Mr. Bremer and Djordjevic before the dramatic events of 9/11).
On September 11, 2001, Mr. Bremer was not in his office. !!!???
This whole plan was revealed in time to the CIA through the now deceased Dr. Milorad G. Markovich.

In *The Serbian Army,* I was regularly publishing images of planes crashing down on the above-mentioned targets.
The CIA did not want to prevent this???
Neither did they want to stop the killing of Shiptars* in Kosovo.
This was not committed by Serbs, but by agents from SION* (I was the karate trainer of SION in Oslo, Norway at the end of 1969 and throughout 1970).
SION agents were also responsible for the massacre in Slavonia.
Furthermore, SION agents were guilty of the massacre in Russia.
Djordjevic - Bremer- Micirevic and company consciously allowed this to happen.

The main center of the Anti-Terrorism group of Mr. Bremer was located in one of the Twin Towers. He had in his treasure vault 40 billion dollars in gold, which was destroyed in the attack by so-called Islamic terrorists. Nothing was recovered on the destroyed Ground Zero.

The gold melted!?

Okay!

So-called anti-terrorist fighters stole 40.000.000.000 US Dollars and now somebody has to pay for that.

Yesterday Serbia!

Today Iraq!

Tomorrow Russia!

Wake up people!!!

This Mr. Bremer is now VESIR in Iraq.

Double agents from the Dutch Secret Service informed me in writing that a certain Palestinian Sheik Houssaini bought 60 kg of plutonium, from Mr. S.F. and Mr. M. (Both were close friends of the brother of [former Dutch] Prime Minister Ruud Lubbers. R. Lupez* is now High Commissioner for Refugees at the UN).

This Sheik Houssaini wanted to make a couple of atomic bombs in order to drop them on Israel so as to revenge the Israeli Secret Agency Mossad for the murder of his son.

The CIA through Djordjevic and Dr. Markovic asked me to sign a false declaration to the effect that Saddam Hussein (and not Sheik Husseini) had bought the plutonium and that he had ordered special fuses for nuclear bombs.

I refused to do so.

Because giving false testimony is a heinous crime!!!

That is all for now, Bajo. I think it is good that you know this. Give a copy of this letter to Mr. Momcilo.

Greetings to you, your family and friends,

Slobodan von Piva, the Avenger.

P.S. A few years ago, I met an old friend from Trebini (Obren). He is married to a woman from Montenegro and told me that he knows you. I asked him to do me a favor by sending you a PC (personal computer), but he did not want to do that.

App. XIV – Letter from Prime Minister Lubbers

Official letter from Dutch Prime Minister R.F.M. Lubbers, dated The Hague, November 2, 1984 to Slobodan Mitric. It was written at the time that Mitric was involved with Lubbers in the Plutonium case dealt with in the next appendices. The letter was published a few years later in his (confiscated) book *Nederland's Mafia* (The Dutch Maffia) and afterwards in *Operation Twins I* . In English it reads as follows: "Dear Mr. Mitric, Your letter from October 19, 1984 concerning 'the exchange of spies', I have received in good order. You can be assured that this matter has my attention, Yours respectfully, (signed) Drs. R.F.M. Lubbers."

MINISTER-PRESIDENT

Nr. 349558

's-Gravenhage, 2 november 1984

Zeer geachte heer Mitric,

Uw brief van 19 oktober 1984 betreffende het onderwerp "ruilen van spion" heb ik in goede orde ontvangen.

U kunt zich ervan verzekerd weten dat de zaak mijn aandacht heeft.

Met de meeste hoogachting,

(Drs. R.F.M. Lubbers)

De heer S.R. Mitric
p/a Mevrouw I. de Wit
Zeeburgerdijk 25
3e zolderetage
1093 SK AMSTERDAM

Appendix XV – Letter by Mitric to Lubbers

Publisher's note: The following letter to former Dutch Prime Minister Lubbers, at that time UN High Commissioner for Refugees in Geneva, was also first published in *Operation Twins I*. It concerns a still sensitive international plutonium and espionage case and came to be written in the following manner.

Sometime in August 2004, I mentioned to Slobodan Mitric that I had been invited to attend a conference on the topic of the relationship between politics and religion by the Dutch political party, the CDA (Christian Democratic Appeal) on September 10 in the town of Utrecht. Since Dr. Lubbers was scheduled to give the closing speech at this conference (subject to change) and since I was aware that Dr. Mitric had "some unfinished business" to do with Dr. Lubbers, I asked Dr. Mitric, if I could do anything for him at this conference.

Dr. Mitric at first suggested I stand up during this conference and confront Dr. Lubbers with his past "wheeling and dealing" regarding the plutonium case that both men apparently had been involved in around 1986. Since I said that this would probably cause my premature, if not forced exit from the said conference site, Dr. Mitric decided to write Dr. Lubbers a letter in Serbian on this "unfinished business". I would then personally hand over this letter to Dr. Lubbers, so as to make sure he would receive it.

This letter in Serbian was subsequently, by mistake, emailed on September 3, 2004 to the Dutch inverstigative journalist Ton Biesemaat in The Hague, together with an answer, also in Serbian, from Dr. Mitric to a request for information. Mr. Biesemaat wanted namely to know Mitric's opinion on a series of inflammatory articles on the internet "De Schaduwkommando van de Prins" (The Shadow Commando of Prince Bernard), in which Dr. Mitric, much to his chagrin, is given a leading role. (…) Ton Biesemaat in any case emailed that he was unable to finance any translations, including the Lubbers letter, all of which probably did not get to him in a legible fashion, because of the Serbian Cyrillic script.

But since there was a slight possibility that Mr. Biesemaat might as yet have gotten access to the Lubbers letter before the recipient Dr. Lubbers himself did, Dr. Mitric found it necessary to fax the letter to his UN Office of in Geneva, which was done from the Willehalm Institute in Amsterdam on or around September 6.

Included were a letter of introduction in Dutch containing an urgent appeal to Dr. Lubbers to respond to the matter at hand (here published in English after the letter by Dr. Mitric) and a number of relevant enclosures.

The handing over of the package with the said letter, the enclosures, a copy of Dr. Mitric's book *De Bijbel van de man zonder geloof* (Bible of the Man Without Faith) with a dedication in Serbian by the author to Dr. Lubbers, as well a Dutch copy of my translation of *The Virtues – Twelve Contemplations On The Months Of The Year* by Herbert Witzenmann, in the end never did take place however, because towards the close of the conference in Utrecht it was announced that Dr. Lubbers was unfortunately unable to deliver his scheduled closing speech.

Until this time of writing, January 6, 2005 [update May 12, 2011] there has been no response whatsoever from Dr. Lubbers to the following letters.

*

K.O.S.A

Dr. Slobodan Von Piva
Zeeburgerdijk 25
1093 SK Amsterdam
Amsterdam, August 29, 2004

Dr. R.F.M. Lubbers
Lambertweg 4
3062 Rotterdam

God Bless You Mister Lubbers,
In the hope that you are doing well, I am taking the liberty to write you a few words.

I suppose you remember who I am, since we had some personal contact in the beginning of the 1980s. Anyways, I want to remind you of some of the things that brought us into contact.

In 1984, some influential people from the Ministry of Justice of the Kingdom of the Netherlands suggested to me and my lawyer Mr. Luc Hammer that I contact you personally and give you the court cases I was charged with, since you were the Prime Minister of the Netherlands and the head of the IDB (*Inlichtingen Dienst Buitenland*, The Dutch Secret Service). It was discovered that all the body of evidence that could help my defense against these charges had mysteriously disappeared. In order to cover up their evil plans and activities in secret nuclear plots, dozens of corrupted persons working for the Ministry of Justice, Ministry of Internal Affairs, and the Army had organized dozens of Dutch prostitutes to support false accusations that I had raped them. As you already know, all the issues at stake concerned dangerous activities of secret organizations that had, and still have, the aim of using nuclear weapons against the USA, Israel, Australia, Canada, and some states of the European Union. Their weapons are: 60 kg highly modified plutonium, 60,000 (sixty thousand) kg of uranium that will be modified to plutonium, several containers of uranium stolen from the storage facilities at *Philips*, dumped into the sea and threatening to cause a severe ecological catastrophe, etc.

As you know, you gave me the orders through your personal assistant Jos Kibom to mediate in the transaction of 60 kg of plutonium of which one part (6 kg) was sold to the Palestinian Sheik Sabaidi Hussein for $500,000,000. You gave the orders personally to the director of the IDB, General Romein, who had hired a state prosecutor in charge of espionage and nuclear threats, Mr. Oos to draw up the agreement with me.

As you must remember, you personally suggested that I should be given a reward for helping to prevent this hideous crime. The reward was supposed to be that I would receive Dutch citizenship and that all false charges against me would be dropped. You [further] agreed that the informer Mr. G. van H., a Dutch citizen and member of the IDB, should be freed of any legal responsibility and be given a reward for his decision to hand in this terrorist organization and remaining plutonium. You agreed to the following terms:

1. To provide Mr. G. van H. with a new identity;
2. To give Mr. G. van H. a reward of 3.000.000 Dutch guilders;
3. To permit Mr. G. van H. to import semi-legal products, worth 5.000.000 guilders from South America, forbidden on the Dutch market only because of the competition;
4. To free Mr. G. van H. from having to pay 5,000,000 guilders worth of taxes;
5. To give me Dutch citizenship – however my lawyer asked you to grant me political asylum instead, in order for me to be able to go legally to the USA – and cover my expenses to the amount of US $ 3,000,000 that I incurred during several years of my investigation and activities against said terrorist organizations as director of Reserve Police International for the Netherlands (as you know, I was directly responsible to the General director of Reserve Police-International general Raymond Healey, former director of the CIA for Europe and Asia).

We had agreed to keep this agreement a top secret of the Kingdom of the Netherlands.
As you know, you were the one and not I, who has broken this agreement and as such never paid a single guilder to me or to the informer.
You are very well informed about the current world situation.
You know very well that you have a personal responsibility for all the missed opportunities to prevent planned terrorist attacks.
At the moment that you were charged with sexual harassment in your department, I saw that God's hand might be slow, but effective.
I am glad that these charges against you were withdrawn, but I am sad to see that you did not fulfil a single part of our agreement.
As you know, from the moment that you broke our agreement, I was at the mercy of the Kingdom of Netherlands and until this very day, I have no legal rights.
I do not have the promised political asylum.
I do not have the promised Dutch citizenship.
I do not have health insurance, besides I have become severely ill from the effect of torture by the Dutch state.
I do not have the right to work.
I do not have social security.

I am asking you through this letter to re-consider our agreement once again and fulfill your part in it, pay for my expenses (of course, with the international interest rate) and allow me to spend the rest of my life working and living like any normal citizen of this country, a country that has been torturing me physically and psychologically now for decades.

Wishing you all the best, and may God give all of us what we deserve.

Respectfully yours,
Dr. Slobodan Radojev Mitric

P.S. – Your wife, Ms. Ria Lubber has still not paid for my book *Nederland's Maffia* and the delivery costs, which she ordered in 1985 trough my wife, the artist Iris Mitric de Vries. Is it part of your family not to pay for your debts and violate agreements?

*

Fax from R.J. Kelder at the Willehalm Institute in Amsterdam
To Dr. R.F.M. Lubbers
United Nations High Commissioner for Refugees
Geneva, Switzerland

Amsterdam, September 6, 2004

Concerns: Dr. Slobodan Von Piva (Mitric)

Dear Dr. Lubbers,
The above-mentioned displaced and stateless fugitive Dr. Slobodan Radojev von Piva, at one time famous if not [undeservedly] infamous here in this country as Karate Bob, has asked me to fax you his letter in the Serbian language with enclosures, which I hereby enact. Since he has translated this letter orally for me, I am aware of its content.
I know Dr. Mitric since 1987 as a noble man, a writer, a monk, a freedom fighter and anti-terrorist, secret agent and field criminologist, who about since that time through various circumstances has landed in a difficult if not increasingly hopeless predicament, which

therefore also indirectly applies to his wife, the artist Iris Mitric-de Vries.

He and his wife have been quite ill for some time already and may not have much more time left to live. In spite of the fact that Dr. Mitric has already been in this nation for some 30 years and in spite of the fact that he has already been married to his Dutch wife for 12 years, he still does not possess a residence permit, let alone the Dutch nationality, even though this and more had been promised to him (apparently also by you) for his services to this State of the Netherlands. He has the status of an undesirable alien, still has no social security, can or may not work, has no medical help for his bodily aches and pains and has officially been sentenced in two shameful show processes as a rapist, through which in the eyes of the Dutch public he appears nota bene as a common criminal.

In short, a case of character assassination and a gross violation of the most fundamental human rights in the Netherlands.

In the course of several years, I have in vain attempted to bring his increasingly desolate living and legal situation to the attention of the authorities and have tried to help him in other ways to survive, let alone enjoy a normal working existence.

By means of this letter, Dr. Mitric has now decided to remind you of a contract that you have apparently once made with him, but that according to Dr. Mitric you did not honor. Furthermore, I understand that he has asked you as yet to live up to this contract.

I strongly urge to deal with this case and to see to it that justice be done and that accordingly Dr. Mitric and his wife can spend the remaining years of their life on earth in a fashion worthy of human dignity. Even without the afore-mentioned contract with Dr. Mitric, you in your present function would have enough reason to do so.

Thanking you in advance, I am,

Yours very respectfully,
Robert J. Kelder
Dir. Willehalm Institute

P.S. Information over my work can be found on: www.willehalm.nl
Enclosures: Letter by Dr. Slobodan Von Piva with enclosures

Appendix XVI

Karate Bob and Prime
Minister Lubbers' Muslim Bomb

**The following article is taken from the Dutch internet site
Kleintje Muurkrant: www.stelling.nl/followup/. Its original title
is "Lubbers en de Muzelmannenbom"; no author was mentioned. It appeared in 12 instalments from September 7 to October 18, 2005 and was first printed in English in the appendix
of *Operation Twins II* as a supplement to the letter published in
the appendix of *Operation Twins I* in which Mitric asks Lubbers
to finally live up to their contract, mentioned below, something
which has not happened to this day (May 12, 2011). The name
of the intermediary between Karate Bob and Lubbers, who was
designated in *Operation Twins I* only by G. van H. and in the
original Dutch internet version of this article by a certain X, was
here, on the authority of Slobodan Mitric, revealed for the first
time: it is Van Hulst, former head of the Dutch BVD (National
Security Service), which in 2002 became the AIVD. This lengthy
article is republished here to document the fact that Slobodan
Mitric as general director of World Atomic Counter-Espionage
(WACE) was indeed involved in high-level secret transactions in
this field.**

It caused but a wrinkle in the [Dutch] mainstream media: Lubbers
pronouncement on August 9 of this year [2005] that the CIA was
informed from the beginning of the activities of the Pakistani metal-
lurgical engineer Abdul Qadeer Khan, the father of the Pakistani
nuclear bomb. And that the Agency preferred to let him go his way;
supposedly, to be able to map his network. Bullshit of course, but
never mind. After a couple of members of the [Dutch Prime Minis-
ter] Balkenende gang declared the ex-premier more or less
whoopee, and Lubbers himself did not come up with more details,
the story disappeared into the archives. In spite of the fact that Ruud
Lubber's story, to which Krista van Velzen from the [Dutch] Parliament had already given a prelude, had a formidable impact. We
felt ourselves in fact nicely ´blubberd´ and not for the first time
either.

We have, as it happens, already referred more often to another
nuclear affair which the womaniser from Kralingen [a suburb of

Rotterdam] has been associated during his political career. In that context he got visit at home from two gentlemen on the evening of January 18, 1985. One of them he knew well. That was Jos Kieboom, his own consultant. He did not know the other one. It was a Rotterdammer, who was acting as an intermediary for the detained Slobodan Mitric, alias Karate Bob. The latter had had been incarcerated in various state institutions during the eighties, where he heard whispers in the grapevine concerning a secret nuclear deal between a business delegation from Dutch industry and a mixed delegation from the Middle East plus in that context the theft of a sizable shipment of uranium.

Mitric claimed to know where that uranium was and sought indirect contact with Prime Minister Lubbers. The latter regarded the matter obviously that serious that he took steps to have Kieboom arrange the afore-mentioned meeting with Mitric's intermediary on January 18, 1985. Out of that meeting came the following list of demands made by Mitric as articulated by his intermediary on January 30:

"Following the delivery and affirmation of the sample, the detention of Mitric is to be suspended immediately. Mitric and persons to be appointed by him are then requested to negotiate at once to formulate their demands to Prime Minister Lubbers. All demands made by me, Van Hulst, being:

A residence permit for Mitric;
Protection for the informant involved;
Bail payment of the agreed amount
are to be met in advance.
With regard to the matter of the presence of representatives of foreign nations, this will be rejected."

No trifle thus, but because the uranium sample was not delivered, the whole matter was eventually dropped. Which does not mean, however that the stolen uranium did not exist.

It would be nice if Lubbers were to also go public concerning this affair. But then preferably from A to Z. Otherwise we continue to guess.

II

The intermediary, Van Hulst, between the then prime minister Lubbers and the detained Slobodan Mitric had not been chosen accidentally. Van Hulst had been, as it happens, from the beginning involved in the afore-mentioned secret negotiations between the delegation of Dutch businessmen and the motley crew from the Middle East concerning the nuclear deal. And – a happy detail – he had arrived on Augusts 4, 1984, because of a minor incident via a police cell in Maassluis, at the house of detention..

After two days, he got a visit from an inspector, named "De Boer", who invited him to work on a large forthcoming project. Now, Van Hulst sat there anyways, you can annoy yourself literally to death in jail, so why not? Within a couple days he got a new neighbour who had been transferred from Leeuwarden [in the Dutch province of Friesland] to Rotterdam. You can bet who that was, very well: Slobodan Mitric.

In the months afterwards, "Bob" Mitric was to confide to his neighbour that he was busy closing a deal with the [Dutch central] Ministry of General Affairs. He wanted to get out of jail in exchange for disclosing the whereabouts of the stolen shipment of uranium. Would Van Hulst act as an intermediary when he got out again? Well, Van Hulst wouldn't't mind.

Two days before the annual hustle and bustle concerning that stable in Bethlehem Van Hulst was freed. The first weeks he heard nothing. But before the first week of January 1985 was over, he got a phone call. If he would care to visit Bob a moment. Of course.

According to the slightly agitated Mitric, the matter would come to a head and Van Hulst would be approached by a couple of chaps who would close the deal. And indeed, that same evening Van Hulst got a phone call. An unknown voice said:*We are the people that Bob was talking about this afternoon. We want to talk with you for a while. If you walk now to the corner of the street, we will pick you up there.*

The intermediary quickly put on his coat, ran to the corner of the street and stepped in a car filled with two men from [The Ministry of] General Affairs. After a short ride, the trio came to the parking lot of a restaurant where the boys from the Ministry explained what they wanted. If Van Hulst would cooperate in solving the matter, which Mitric had brought forward. Van Hulst hesitated, but the boys from the Ministry are known for their power of persuasion and Van Hulst finally came around. After he was brought back home, one of the men said
In two hours you will receive a telephone call.

And he was right. About twelve o'clock the phone rang: *With Kieboom. If you to go to Erasmus university tomorrow morning, you*

131

will find me on the first floor at the Donner bookshop. There we can talk further.

III

Any doubts that Van Hulst, the intermediary of Slobodan Mitric, might have had about his appointment with Jos Kieboom were entirely eliminated the next morning. He found Lubbers' consultant indeed on the agreed spot: the Donner bookshop on the first floor of Erasmus University. WhetherVan Hulst at that moment already knew what kind of function Kieboom held, remains a question. After some obligatory preliminaries, the two gentlemen withdrew to a parlour. There Van Hulst unrolled the list of demands by Mitric that, in his view of the slow course the negotiations, had been modified repeatedly in the preceding period.

Kieboom listened to Van Hulst and said patiently at the end of the conversation: *Well, I know it now. Wait a while longer. I will call you again and then I'll take you to someone.*

A few of days later, on Saturday January 18, at the end of the afternoon, the intermediary got Kieboom on the line, who asked him if he could be at the Kralinger golf club at seven o'clock. There he would come by to pick up Van Hulst.

Properly on time, the two men met each other again. This time at the parking lot of the golf club. Kieboom: *Now I will bring you to someone with whom you can definitively close the deal.*

They drove through the better part of Kralingen to a villa on the corner of Lambertweg and walked in the dark along the garden path to the front door, which opened almost immediately. Before he knew it, Van Hulst stood in the study on the first floor. Together with Kieboom. A moment later the occupant of the house made his appearance: Ruud Lubbers, the prime minister. And the conversation began.

IV

The basic list of demands made by Slobodan Mitric was rather simple: official pardon after delivery of the sample of uranium, a residence permit, protection for the original informant and the deposit of three millions dollar in a Swiss bank with a down payment of 1 million. Furthermore, the intermediary requested Lubbers to find out if the British could possibly "take Mitric over" in matters of housing him and a job with some British secret service. If London agreed to this, Mitric would like to see that confirmed in an advertisement of [the biggest Dutch daily newspaper] "De Telegraph".

Lubbers did not find this a nice idea immediately. Also, the proposal to set Mitric free in exchange for information did not fall immediately into place. But after some insistence, he said with his eyes squeezed: *Ah, I don't have to take care of that. But I know some people who are perhaps interested in his knowledge and they have enough power to secure his future.*

Eventually, Lubbers even agreed to place an ad in [the Dutch daily] "De Telegraaf", if the wishes of Mitric could be fulfilled. The text of it read:

"F. Giesberts must take the place of Martin. Sorry about half joker. This was fateful for him. The BIG INDUSTRIALIST wants to first read the book of 239 pages before it is definitively published. F. Giesberts has half the bait already. The vassal of the big industrialist has the other half. M.Amman and film star, as a matter of fact also a big madam, sit in the editorial commission. Don't worry. You were and remain a loner.
Your friend, Frank Waterfort."

Cryptic, but not unbreakable. M. Amman stood for the Israeli military intelligence service, the film star for president Reagan, the big madam for premier Thatcher and the big industrialist for Lubbers. The book of 239 pages was "The Dutch Mafia" that Mitric had conceived [should be "Operation Twins" according to Mitric, note by the translator]. But who was Martin, who according to the text apparently went around the corner [i.e. died] previously, because he possessed the half joker?

Logically that could only be one: Martinus Fens, who was murdered on December 17, 1984. Alias "beautiful Tinus", the uncrowned king of the underworld in The Hague and the protagonist in Mitric' masterwork [The Dutch Mafia, not translated].

V

As mentioned in this series, Slobodan Mitric gathered his knowledge concerning the shipment of uranium, which floated around somewhere, as well as the nuclear deal between a delegation of Dutch businessmen and a mixed party from the Middle East, in his round of penitentiaries. But especially in Esserheem, where also Tinus Fens, the king of the underworld at that time in The Hague, was jailed for smuggling drugs.

In the early spring of 1984, beautiful Tinus was released. Apparently everyone did not find that so amusing, because in May of that year he was shot in Café Petit Paris in The Hague by a couple of young hit-men. Tinus was a tough guy. He survived the attack. But on December 17, the bell nevertheless tolled for him. A North-African shot him from nearby through the back of his head.

According to newspapers from that time, the gunman had been engaged by two other toppers from the scene in The Hague: porno-king Henkie Bartels and gambling expert Henk Rijstenbil. During interrogation and the following trial, both the gunman and Rijstenbil denied all charges leveled at them. They both had nothing to do with the murder. Bartels sang like a canary. Consequence: Bartels and Rijstenbil went behind bars for a long time. The North-African was allowed to leave for lack of proof.

A couple months after the sentence, Bartels was sent home because of his frail health. That appeared to be in Thailand where he spent five years before he departed to higher spheres.

The question remains whether the death of Tinus Fens resulted indeed simply from a power struggle between him and the duo Bartels/Rijstenbil or whether the scenario was a lot more complicated. A scenario in which the nuclear question with which Mitric was playing joker also had a role. Perhaps something at this late date for Rijstenbil's lawyer Gerard Spong.

VI

In order to keep the pressure on, Mitric, after the visit by intermediary Giesberts on January 21 sent a letter to the house address of premier Lubbers with duplicates to the American, British, French and Israeli embassies. The contents read as follows:

"Your Excellency,

In the first place [I send you] my best wishes for the new year. By means of this letter, I want to turn to you with some questions. The contents of this matter could damage you if they are not true. For this reason, I have decided do let to this matter come directly to you. It is not in my interests to cause you harm in any way.

1. Have you ordered in December 1983 an investigation into the theft of uranium?

If yes:

a. Have you ordered the intelligence service of the Ministry of General Affairs to speak with me on your behalf in January 1984 concerning this matter?

b. Did the civil servant of the intelligence service of your ministry, Mr. Mansveld, have to negotiate with me on your behalf from January 1984 until July 20, 1984?

2. Did you order De Telegraaf to place the following small add on your behalf on June 19, 1984?

"Martin, your half joker is worth as much as my half joker. The big industrialist is very much interested in putting our jokers together. Greetings from Koos".

If yes:

a. Did you know that by placing this ad, you agreed to my conditions?

The big industrialist is your code name, known at the Intelligence Service of General Affairs as well as by my informant in whose name I have done the complete transaction with you.

b. Conditions were:

1. That I would be granted the Dutch nationality.

2. That I would be paid 3 million US dollar, 1 million cash in advance to me (that I would be allowed to bring to Switzerland) and the rest by means of a written guarantee by a notary. Plus half a million guilders cash for the first kilo uranium.

3. From you the written guarantee that I would never be extradited to Yugoslavia against my will.

4. From you the written guarantee that I will never be prosecuted for this affair.

5. That all the debts that my informant owes in taxes are remitted (about 10 million guilders).

6. That the name of my informant will never be made public.

7. That my informant be given a complete new identity.

8. Permission for the import of goods, for this one time only, that are prohibited in The Netherlands. This is important, because these goods are used as payment by countries in the Middle East.

The detection of these goods serves as additional evidence.

As you know, by placing the above ad, you agreed to all the conditions.

3. Is it true that the following decision was made at an emergency meeting on July 20:

a. That you as Prime Minister (also minister of General Affairs) agreed to start the transaction with me?

b. That the minister of Foreign Affairs also agreed to my conditions?

c. That the minister of Justice did not agree?

Conclusion: That the whole affair was covered up as a result of the negative position of the minister of Justice as enacted by his advisors, among others the public prosecutor Mr. Van Os? The risk that this uranium will fall into enemy hands and be used against the state of Israel will then be entirely your responsibility. Not to forget the 10 barrels of radio-active waste that were stolen from Philips-Eindhoven and that are in danger of being sold to the IRA.

4. Do you know F. Giesberts?
5. Was F. Giesberts with you at the end of December 1984?
a. Did you permit police commissioner Blaauw to speak about the uranium issue with the Intelligence Services of General Affairs?
b. Did you grant him full powers to deal with me in future negotiations?
c. Did you receive from Mr. F. Giesberts the text of the ad that was to be placed in the section Small Ads of De Telegraaf?

"F. Giesberts must take the place of Martin. Sorry about half joker. This was fateful for him. The BIG INDUSTRIALIST wants to first read the book of 239 pages before it is definitively published. F. Giesberts has half the bait already. The vassal of the big industrialist has the other half. M. Amman and film star, as a matter of fact also a big madam, sit in the editorial commission. Don't worry. You were and remain a loner.
Your friend,
Frank Waterfort."

We know the identity of intermediary Giesberts as well as that of Mitric's informant, but for the time being see no need to reveal their names.

VII

If we can believe the data from the letter Slobodan Mitric wrote to prime minster Lubbers dated January 21,1985 then the stolen uranium affair and – be it to a lesser degree – the secret negotiations on Cyprus lasted more than a year. From December 1983 to in any case January 1985.

Quite soon after his first edict to General Affairs (GA), Mitric, according to the same data in the Schevening house of detention, was visited by an agent from IDB [Dutch CIA] operating under GA. It was Koos Mansveld, who introduced himself to Mitric as Mansfield. During the next months agent Mansfield would visit his detained informant numerous times. First in Scheveningen and after March 27, 1984 in the cupola [jail with domed roof] in Haarlem.

Those visits must have given the Montenegrin karate expert the impression that his information was taken seriously by the IDB. Question is whether the above sketch of events is a figment of the imagination of the caged ex-agent of Tito or the naked truth. The latter. This we can distil from a report of a staff member of the Haarlem detention center that he wrote at the end of July 1984, when Mitric was transferred to Leeuwarden. In that report, intended for his colleagues in the Frisian capital, he wrote, among other things, the following:

"During his stay here, the person concerned attracted the interest of the foreign intelligence service, operating under the ministry of General Affairs. Mr. Mansfield, a member of this service [IDB], paid him numerous visits. This all happened in consultation with Mr. Van Hylkema and Mr. Van Os, Public prosecutor in The Hague."

We asked the RVD [Public Relations Office of the Kingdom of The Netherlands] concerning this affair. The then head of this Office, also operating under GA, Hans van der Voet, admitted to our enormous surprise that a civil servant from GA had indeed visited Mitric. Further, he do not want go. Van der Voet: *I can only say to you that it is true.*

VIII

Not long after his detailed letter to Lubbers dated January 20, 1985 the sleuths called in by GA came to the conclusion that Mitric heard a nuclear bell ringing, but did not know exactly where the clapper was. That was sufficient to lower the storm flag and proceed to damage control. In other words, eliminating loose cannon Mitric. For example, during the appeal that the furious karate man had made in a law suit that three women had filed against him because of rape. Remarkable detail: one of the women was the former wife of Mitric' informant in the uranium affair.

The ex-agent of Tito vehemently denied the charges and claimed that it was a plot by the government in order to keep him behind bars and in this way to prevent him from bringing anything concerning the uranium affair into the open. For this reason, it was not astonishing that his lawyer at that time, Mr. H.C.W.F. Meijer in September of that year tried to place a number of persons on the witness list who were not directly involved with the [so-called] rape of the three ladies. They were successively:

"Dr. R.F.M. Lubbers, Lambertweg 4, Rotterdam.
He can explain that he in his function as minister-president in or around December 1983 ordered the Foreign Intelligence Service [IDB] operating under the ministry of General Affairs to contact S. Mitric, that he personally followed this contact, that he also ordered an investigation into the person of S. Mitric, that his ministry of General Affairs on the basis of the results of this research became convinced that afore-mentioned S. Mitric did not commit these rapes and that he then in or around January 1985 through F. Giesberts got in touch again with S. Mitric; Mansfield (initials unknown), at least a person who used this name as his own, c/o Executive Board Foreign Intelligence Service [IDB] Plein 20, The Hague.
He can explain that he was ordered by Dr. R.F.M. Lubbers, mentioned under a, to investigate the theft of a certain amount of plutonium, that he therefore approached S. Mitric and then established multiple contacts concerning this affair, that he came with S. Mitric to a sort of transaction, according to which S. Mitric was promised, among other things, money, acquisition of the Dutch nationality, at least a refugee passport, a guarantee against deportation from the territory of the Kingdom of the Netherlands, protection of S. Mitric against possible reprisals and an investigation into the rape charges levelled against S. Mitric;

Dr. J.P. Kieboom, Zeekant 99f, The Hague.
He can explain that he in or around the months of November and December 1983 was approached on behalf of S. Mitric, that he then established contact with Dr. R.F.M. Lubbers, that the latter on the advice of Kieboom entered into proposals by Mitric and that an amount of 300,000,000 West-German marks was lent by the Dutch government to the Palestinian Hassan Sabaidi;

Mr. F.G.J. of Os, Barnsteenhorst 370, The Hague.
He can explain that and why he attempted in an unlawful manner to put pressure on S. Mitric' lawyer at that time, Mr. L.D.H. Hammer, why he advised Dr. R.F.M. Lubbers to make no appointments with S. Mitric, that he said to be able prove that the

statements by S. Mitric were at variance with the truth, that he ordered S. Mitric to be liquidated in the house of detention in Leeuwarden and that he called S. Mitric a rapist;

Mr. H.W. of Hylkema, Princess Margrietlaan 17, Voorburg. He can explain that he advised Dr. R.F.M. Lubbers to maintain no further contact with S. Mitric, that he knew that S. Mitric was a rapist - or, in case he did not know this, that and why he has nevertheless stated this - and that he ordered the liquidation of S. Mitric in the house of detention in Leeuwarden;

Mr. G.P.H. van Doeveren, Norgstraat 67, The Hague. He can explain that he set the detained H. de Wolf in or around august 1983 free and why he did this, that he advised Dr. R.F.M. Lubbers to presuppose that S. Mitric was a liar, and that the amount of uranium and plutonium that Mitric was talking about was 'worthless stuff', that he called S. Mitric a rapist and that by all odds he incited women to level rape charges against S. Mitric."

Although for Mitric, plutonium and uranium were apparently one and the same thing, there remains sufficient material to scratch yourself firmly behind the ears. Liquidation orders. A mysterious loan to Hassan Sabaidi? What was that all about?

Of course, you will hasten to say, the above-mentioned witnesses were not summoned. According to the presiding judge of the law court Wedeven and solicitor general Ficq, they had absolutely nothing to do with the rape case. In spite of the fact that the desired high profile witnesses stayed away, Mitric nevertheless tried during the court session to establish a link between the rape affair and the uranium matter. To no avail. He lost the case and remained behind bars. Which does not mean that the uranium matter was shelved and that it indeed concerned worthless stuff.

IX

As has been said, the relation between Mitric and the Foreign Intelligence Service [IDB] operating under Lubbers' Ministry of General Affairs lasted more than one year. But how did that relation come about? That was through a letter, which the ex-agent of Tito sent to the turret [Prime Minister Lubbers' parliamentary office in The Hague] and which contains the following moving strophes:

An international organisation which consists exclusively of Islamic, well-situated fanatics aims at all costs to construct a number of nuclear bombs and to have them explode on the territory of Israel. This organisation had nothing except money. Therefore it was forced to look for experts abroad. This way they came into contact with some Dutch and Belgian businessmen. Thus the plan construed by these fanatics slowly took shape. The organisation started by buying the raw materials necessary for the production of nuclear bombs.

They bought in the USA: 600 kilos of Uranium-235, in Switzerland five bars of Uranium-235 and in Belgium five bars of Uranium-235.

Furthermore they bought ten barrels of mass necessary for the creation of the nuclear link. Later it appeared that this mass was nothing else than radioactive waste, stolen from Philips-Eindhoven.

In June/July 1981, a meeting took place on the island of Cyprus between the party giving the orders and the contractors. At that meeting were present:

   A member of the secret service of Syria

   A member of the secret service of Lybia

   A Jordan-Palestinian oil-sheik

   A civil servant of the Dutch Ministry of Foreign Affairs (double agent Warschau Pact)

   A Dutch businessman (as of now code name Giesberts)

   A nuclear physicist/engineer of Italian origin

   A chemist/engineer or nuclear physicist from the Middle East

This meeting was top secret. The following was decided. Because all the material that the organisation had until then bought was not suited for making a nuclear bomb, an advance of 20 million dollar was paid to buy proper material. With that money, 60 kilos Uranium-238 (99.3 percent) were bought in Belgium. The leader of the group who provided this U-238 is an ex-minister of the Belgian government. The transaction between purchasers and salesmen was arbitrated by a civil servant from [the Ministry] of Foreign Affairs and Giesberts.

Interesting is that during the meeting on Cyprus the aim behind the purchase of uranium was discussed: making a couple of nuclear bombs and to let them explode in Israel and Great Brit-

ain. Giesberts became scared, but he could no longer go back. Giesberts sought contact with me and asked for advice in finding a way out. After I had given Giesberts the guarantee that I would never against his will say anything to third parties, he told me everything. We then agreed that I would negotiate on his behalf with the Dutch government.

F. Giesberts can provide:

> **The complete identity of all persons involved**
> **60 kilos of U-238**
> **10 barrels of radioactive debris**
> **An illegal nuclear laboratory within the Benelux**

According to F. Giesberts the organisation giving the orders has paid, after 20 million dollar in advance in 1982, another 100 million in the form of:

a. Money. Hidden in the diplomatic luggage of a very well-known Dutch lawyer and transported by the aforementioned civil servant of Foreign Affairs.

b. A number of transports of 10,000 kilos hash-hisch;

c. A number of transports of 15,000 kilos marihuana;

d. A number of transports of 50 kilos heroin;

Total wholesale trade value 100 million dollar.

Gold valued at 250 million dollar. This has been not yet transferred to the salesmen (ex-minister Belgium). It is held in an African country.

Remarkable concoction, from which in any case it appears that the makers did not know too much concerning the enrichment procedure of uranium and the difference between U-238 and U-235. Moreover, it is clear that Mitric and the enigmatic Giesberts had known each other earlier than was suggested in part 2 of this series.

But for the rest, there were nevertheless a couple of tasty meat balls in the soup. Lubbers thought that obviously too and sent agent Mansfield to the jug to see if Mitric had more enticing things to tell. And that he had.

X

Mitric told a lot about Fens, at that time king of the scene in The Hague. Part of it he had drawn from the tales of someone who maintained close contact with beautiful Tinus: Frans de Wit, alias Papa Blanca. A contractor who had also had some amorous affairs with Dame Justitia from which he did not escape completely intact. One of his customers was supposedly Hollandia Kloos. A company of the family Lubbers that was governed by Ruud and Rob. [1]

That did not mean that Papa could not only live for a while on state costs, but that he had to cough up some ten million to pay premiums and tax money. Correct. De Wit was Mitric' informant in the uranium issue. And not to forget in the background of the affair: the secret negotiations between a delegation of Dutch businessmen and the not so lively club from the Middle East. And what Mitric came know, Tinus Fens had already known for a long time. As already related in part 5 of this series, during the investigations of the IDB-agent Koos Mansveld and other sleuths, initiated by prime minister Lubbers, Fens was shot twice for his job. The last attack, on December 17, 1984, he did not survive (see part 5).

Oddly enough earlier that year, on 28 Augusts, another intimate of Mitric who was aware of the two hazardous affairs, died suddenly. That was Kurt Görlitz, a prominent member of a secret organisation under the guidance of Hans Teengs Gerritsen, the bosom friend of prince Bernhard (see above all part VI of the "De schaduwkommando van de Prins" on www.stelling.nl/morgenster, a series that was also to be found on the [now closed] website of the slain Theo van Gogh "De gezonde roker"). That same week Mitric was transferred to Leeuwarden. In spite of his loud protests. Mitric was afraid that he would be assassinated there on orders of a couple of big shots at the Ministry of Justice (see part VIII of this series).

To remain in the same sphere: on November 20, 1983 Cor Beets, owner of the largest Café for stolen goods in Amsterdam, De Metro, was murdered in his house above his business. Two Yugoslavians and an adventurous inhabitant from De Rijp, a rural village in North Holland, were apprehended. Although the murder weapon in the house of the Yugoslav in Purmerend was found, the trio, because of lack of proof, were shortly thereafter able to sniff fresh air again. According to the moustached chaps from the Central Research Information Service (CRI) who were regularly tapping Cor's telephone and his business connections, Beets was, together with Braspenninx (a living legend in the smuggler world of that time), busy with an "enormous deal". This concerned a shipment of uranium that was stored in the port of Antwerp (see part 9 for Mitric'

---

[1] Ruud and Rob Lubbers took care of the daily chores of the firm, until Ruud became Prime Minister at the end of 1982. From that moment on Rob alone became the boss, but rumor has it that his brother Paul, who lived just across the Belgian border, also had his fingers in the pot..

references to the role played by a Belgian ex-minister and a party of businessmen in the uranium affair). A slightly bloody tale. Time for more cheerful news.

<h1 style="text-align:center">XI</h1>

If there was one person exactly aware of the ins and outs of the nuclear affair in which Slobodan Mitric was to play a temporary role, then this must have been Giesberts. In the article "Steekspel rond een uranium-deal" (Duel Over an Uranium Deal) on the web-site "De morgenster", it is described how the man, who in January 1985 placed the demands of the Montenegrenian karate master on the table in Lubbers' home, got involved in this not so stringy affair. How through mega-conman Guido Haak in Lebanon he got to know the Palestinian businessman Hassan Zubaidi. And later also his partner Rifat Assad, the then head of the Syrian Secret Service and uncle of the current Syrian president. That was in Cyprus. Because both Zubaidi and Assad were from the beginning part of the Middle-Eastern delegation at the successive secret discussions with the delegation of Dutch businessmen, who were mentioned by Mitric in his letters to Prime Minister Lubbers.

We have never managed to find out exactly which Dutch companies (besides Ballast Nedam and Hollandia Kloos, which were mentioned by Giesberts) all wanted to lick the pot of the planned enrichment deal with Urenco in the form of compensation orders. But in our laborious dialogues in the course of years with the Dutch intermediary, however, two names fell of chaps, who were heading the greedy Dutch club: Van Schaik and Lubbers.

Concerning the question which Van Schaik it was, Giesberts was less explicit, but eventually it became clear that it must have been the engineer J.J. van Schaik, not an unknown at both Royal Shell and the Amsterdam engineering office Comprimo. Comprimo? Correct. The same company that in the same years played a secret role in the laying of the nuclear playing field of Dr. Qadeer Khan in Pakistan.

Also concerning the question which Lubbers was on the field in Cyprus, Giesberts was little accommodating. We suggested Rob, but Giesberts named the name of Paul at a single occasion (see footnote). Too bad, but because of Giesberts' understandable reservation, we have not been able to really answer this question.

Van Schaik and Lubbers were supported on Cyprus by a nice battery of experts. It was after all not peanuts. In this type of deals, it was not possible those years for Iran, for whom the enriched uranium was intended and which lay heavily under fire, to simply transfer the bread to The Netherlands and leave it at that. A most charming scheme of compensation orders was thus concocted for a whole range of Dutch firms that would receive amounts much larger than normal. What would happen to the surplus amounts is easy to guess.

That the phased negotiations did not run smoothly is an understatement.

Giesberts: *It wasn't easy. At a certain moment Van Schaik could stand it no longer. He yelled: 'What am I supposed to do in heaven's name?' After internal consultation, he decided to let everything rebound. Panic naturally. The meeting was adjourned, but nevertheless continued after a while. After both sides had consulted the home front, it was possible to close a new deal. We had some very nerve-racking moments.*

Do we have but one source for this charade on Cyprus? No, two. The other one will come next.

XII

Truck driver Cor J. turned nothing down. This way he performed during his impressive career not only logistically high calibre feats for the Italian mafia, but just as cheerfully took to the road for Mossad or Dutch businesses. Just to name a few: In first half of the seventies, he worked for the freight carrier Frans Maas, nowadays listed on the [Dutch] stock exchange, but around 1976 he stepped over to the transport company Stoof in Breda. Not long afterwards the following transpired:

Cor: It must have been in 1977 when I drove parts of a nuclear reactor to Portugal. With a double semi-trailer and two cranes.
KM: How did you know that they were parts of a nuclear reactor?
Cor: That was written in the papers.
KM: Do you know what the destination was?
Cor: No, I don't know. I had to pick up that cargo in the port of Rotterdam and transport it to an open area in the port of Lisbon. That transport was accompanied by a whole swarm of Dutchmen in inconspicuous cars. According to me, they were boys of the Royal Engineers, because they knew damn well what they were doing. It was, however, a long ride. With a double semi-trailer and such a heavy cargo you don't get anywhere terribly fast. But those boys had permits for the complete route. Nowhere underway did we have any difficulties.

KM: Was it because of this haul that were approached later for that odd job on Cyprus?

Cor: I think so. They knew about it in any case. But I was not engaged immediately to go to Cyprus. That came later. First I attended a couple meetings in hotel Gascogne in Eindhoven and a hotel in Antwerp.

KM: Do you still know who were there?

Cor: I remember that there was a German captain of a coaster. But that's all. I had stowed away my papers in my box, but they were been pinched. I remember that Mr. Diepenbroek of Trénité van Doorne was involved in this matter and a lawyer's office from Rotterdam by the name of Sjollema. After that I was in Cyprus a couple of times.

KM: How many people were involved?

Cor: Always at least some thirty males. Arabs, Italians.

KM: You do you remember who was in control on the Dutch side? Van Schaik? Lubbers?

Cor: Van Schaik says nothing me, but there was a Lubbers present.

KM: Which Lubbers? Rob? Paul?

Cor: No idea at all.

KM: Did you know that it concerned a nuclear matter?

Cor: Yes, naturally. It concerned the transport of a large cooling system.

KM: Did it go through?

Cor: That I don't know, because I was caught in a smuggling job. And I got a visit from three gentlemen from Mossad.

KM: ?????

Cor: I was fishing from the Beemsterbrug [bridge in Purmerend, North Holland]. They said that I had to stop with that job; otherwise some nasty things would happen. I told them then that I had also done some things for Mossad and that they could confirm that in Amsterdam, at the consulate. But they knew that. Therefore, it remained a warning. But I did get scared as hell.

Two witnesses thus for the "Cyprus project" that was handled in 1984/1985 by Slobodan Mitric and for Prime Minister Lubbers reason to send IDB agents in the field. Very likely in order to prevent further leaks. Stay tuned.

Published by The Willehalm Press in 2006

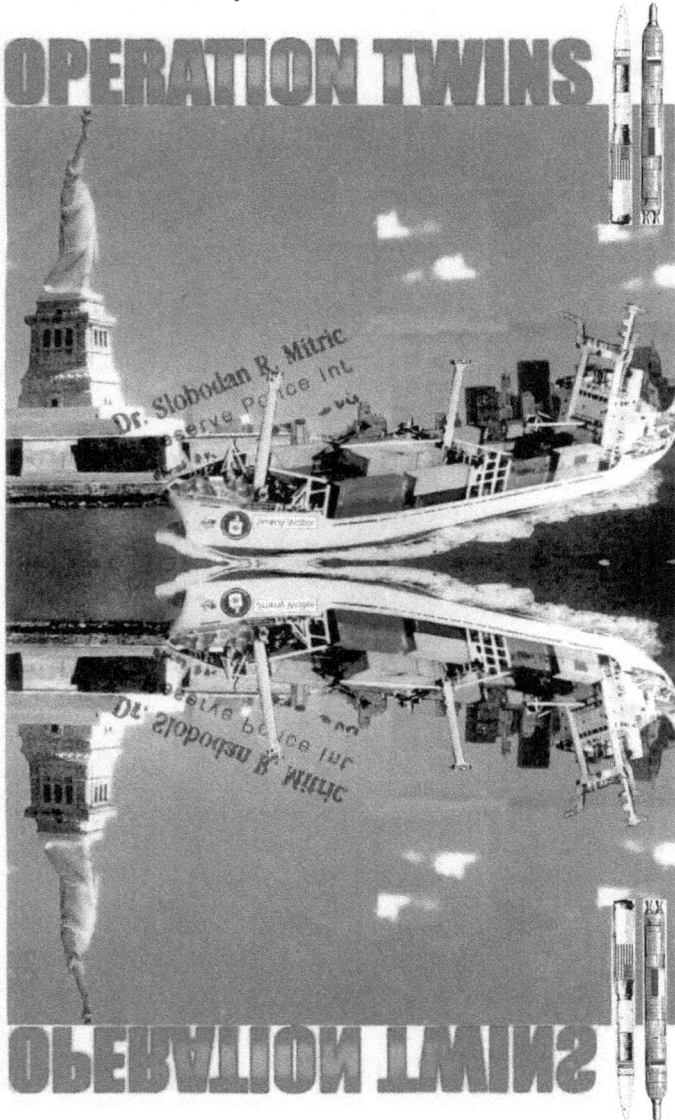

Appendix XVIII – Flap Text *Operation Twins II*

This second edition of the pre-publication of *Operation Twins II* is a sequel to *Operation Twins I* that was published in March 2005 by the Willehalm Institute Press in Amsterdam. In this first volume, it was stated that *Operation Twins* II and III were in the eighties of the last century confiscated by the CIA as containing top secret and highly classified matters relating to both the USSR and the USA.

In this pre-publication, an appeal is made to members of the US Senate and House of Representatives to return these literary works to its rightful owner: the Serbian author, filmmaker and former Yugoslav Secret Agent Slobodan Radojev Mitric (Karate Bob), who has been living and working in virtual exile in Amsterdam for the last 33 years.

The updated material in this pre-publication is based on notes from the original lost version and consist of a summary entitled "The Invisible War Between the 'Secret Services' of America and Russia" and a chapter called "The Titans", including a scene in which the boarding of a nuclear bomb from an underwater base is prevented by the sudden arrival of a US Navy destroyer. New are the 11 appendices. These include an open letter by the author to his nephew Boris Tadic, the current President of Serbia; a Serbian newspaper article on the exploits and expected expulsion of this "Super Agent"; an article "Karate Bob and Lubbers' Muslim Bomb" in which the name of his intermediary is revealed; letters from his former CIA contact Milorad Markovich on his past counter-intelligence and anti-terrorist field work; excerpts from *Operation Twins I* and Mitric' journal The *Serbian Army* related to his forewarnings of 9/11, and two verdicts from 1986 forbidding the Dutch government to expel the author to his home country for fear that his life will be in grave danger there. In spite of the fact that he and others firmly consider this still to be the case, the immigration officials under former BVD (National Security Service) head Mrs. Verdonk of the Dutch department of Justice (recently relieved from her function) gave him thirty days in March of this year (2006) to leave the country. Public protest and an outcry from human rights authorities (temporarily) prevented his expulsion, but a legal appeal to finally obtain a residence permit was lost.

In his updated introduction the publisher gives the reasons for entitling it "Confronting Jimmy Walter and Beyond, Part II" and also draws attention to the legal predicament of his ailing author, who in spite of his many existential trials and tribulations (including recent attacks on his life) has not stepped down from his penetrating counter-intelligence and anti-terrorist work as world director of *Reserve Police International*, part of which is revealed here for the first time.

Willehalm Institute Press, Amsterdam,
ISBN: 978-90-73932-07-4
www.willehalm.nl/ot2.html

"Far From the Beaten Track, Wolves Howl –
A Hunter Hears Them"

The Invisible War Between The "Secret Services" Of America and Russia

On December 31, 2007 two freighters with nuclear warheads on board are sailing in the waters of New York City and St Petersburg. The captains of both ships are unaware of the real cargo in the containers, just as they were for decades unaware of the fact that their crews were illegally transporting tons of narcotics. Exactly at midnight, terrorists infiltrate the ships, open the containers and activate the nuclear warheads.

As may be known, Operation Twins was – if we exclude the attacks by airplanes on the World Trade Center in New York City – partly postponed until further orders. International terrorism has in the mean time spread all over the globe. The Cold War has been suspended for the time being; the super-powers, the United States and Russia, together with their mutual satellite mini-states, have agreed to join forces in the war on terrorism.

Communists from one side and nationalists from the other, however, are absolutely incapable of abiding by this agreement, which they regard as high treason. The aim of these two groups, the so-called 'reds' and 'blues', was and still is to gain complete world domination. The most orthodox factions of both the reds and the blues are prepared to use all available ways and means to throw the momentary status quo of the super-powers off balance, i.e. to completely destroy their adversary.

During the Cold War era both super-powers made plans to emerge some fateful day as the winner of that war. Towards that end, the Secret Services of both blocs developed professional programs and engaged various individuals and groups to work for them.

This book, *Operation Twins II*, reveals in detail the hidden, underground activities of the Secret Services of both super-powers. With the end of the Cold War, the architects of these dark schemes became in fact unemployed. However, they refused to accept their fate.

Underwater bunkers, once used for drug smuggling, were turned into underground storage depots for nuclear weapons of both blocs. Everyone with sufficient money was able to buy all the necessary attributes for the construction of nuclear bombs. Hundreds of top nuclear physicists were sold like football stars with the guaranty that they were capable of constructing a nuclear bomb for everyone possessing the necessary funds. A division of the Dutch mafia named "Titans" controls 90% of the remaining nuclear arsenal from the Cold War.

In one of the underwater bunkers there are no less than two complete nuclear bombs taken from the hulls of US military jet planes that had been shot down. These weapons of mass destruction were traced and recovered by professional divers under the command of a Dutch gangster and former double agent for the Netherlands and Egypt named Hank and a mysterious multi-millionaire from the US.

Operation Twins II further reveals that the Dutch mafia exercises control over 90% of the international terrorists, since it has remained partners with them in the business of smuggling heroin, cocaine, hashish, marijuana, and all similar types of narcotics.

Operation Twins II brings into the open the total, invisible war of the Secret Services between former enemies, now turned "allies". At least one hundred NATO double agents were cut into pieces (in the Dutch region of "Het Gooi") and devoured by lions, leopards, tigers, crocodiles and pigs.

All this is very well known by the leading Dutch politicians and officials, but because of the fact that some of them have been bribed, some blackmailed, and since others are afraid that the nuclear weapons on board of one of the ships might be activated to explode in some Dutch seaport, these details have been withheld from the general public.

Shall *Operation Twins II* be able to prevent new catastrophes that could lead to World War Three and total destruction, just as *Operation Twins I* successfully prevented and postponed the dark plans of these non-humans in 1999? This is up to the commitment of every person in helping *Operation Twins II* see the light of day before it is too late.

Dr. Slobodan Radojev Mitric von Piva

Appendix XX – CV Slobodan Mitric

DOCUMENTED CURRICULUM VITAE OF SLOBODAN R. MITRIC

1948 – Born on March 1 in Vojvodina, northern Serbia
1965 – Writes a play *The Little Pickpocket* and a collection of poems *The Granddad of my Granddad Black Karmatovic* (seized by the Yugoslav Secret Service UDBA).
1968 – Karate and jiu-jitsu trainer of Yugoslav counter-intelligence service CBOB and U.S. marines in Belgrade.
1969 – Karate coach of West German and Swiss secret services.
1970 – Karate coach of the Norwegian Royal Guard, the Norwegian National Karate Team and the NATO intelligence service (SION) in Oslo.
1970 – MI6 and the CIA in Oslo make a karate film of Mitric.
1971- Karate coach of the Swedish intelligence SEPO and IB, the Stockholm Karate Club and the Military Academy in Uppsala, Sweden; disarms the Croatian secret agent and skyjacker Tomislav Rebrina.
1972 – Arrested in Sweden on false charges of assault and rape. Writes the novel *The Belgrade Underworld* (seized by the Secret Service of Yugoslavia, SDB). Appointed head of special operations dept. of Reserve Police-International (RPI) for the Benelux and Scandinavia.
1973 – Survives a liquidation attempt in Sweden by the Yugoslav Secret Service (SDB). Attacked by the SDB in Belgrade by some twenty secret agents and thugs. Refuses to carry out a state liquidation of the Secretary-General of Marxist-Leninist Party of Yugoslavia and head of the KGB in Europe, the Montenegrin immigrant Dapsevic in Brussels; during a subsequent shoot-out in Amsterdam, in which 17 shots are fired at him from a Thomson submachine gun, three of his Yugoslavs assailants are killed and two wounded. Defects to the West. Subsequent attempts to emigrate to the US fail, because of character assassination by the Dutch government.
1974 – Sentenced to 13 years imprisonment for alleged triple murder. Only after three years does the Dutch government reluctantly recognize the assassins were politically motivated. At times allowed to move freely in and out of jail; other times held in maximum security under inhuman conditions.

1976 – In jail writes *Murder Machine of Belgrade* (confiscated by the CIA).

1979 – Publishes in Serbian under the name Zoran Jovanovic ten episodes of a novella called *Confessions of a Disgruntled Spy* in the London-based Yugoslav political-cultural magazine *Nasa Rec*.

1979 – Transferred to a maximum-security prison in Veenhuizen.

1981 – Publishes from jail in Dutch *The Big Karate Book of Karate Bob*, makes karate movie *The Karate Bob*; becomes director and chief editor of the magazine *Karate Europe*. Presents list of 100 double agents to U.S. Ambassador Paul Bremer in The Hague.

1982 – Becomes co-owner and director of dozens of sport shops in Benelux and co-owner and director of the sport machines factory Adonis. Appointed director for the Netherlands of Reserve Police-International founded and based in Tucson, Arizona. Writes in Serbian the "science-fiction" thriller in three parts *Operation Twins* as a basis for a feature film (Parts 2 and 3 later confiscated by the CIA). Publishes in Dutch *Tito's Secret Agent* and *Tito's Murder Machine*. Transferred to solitary confinement in a jail in Rotterdam.

1983 – Sentenced to 5 years imprisonment for alleged rapes of prostitutes. Admission by prostitutes that they were paid to issue these false charges are neglected by his lawyer…

1984 – Publishes a play *Bible of the Man without Faith* that is staged in prison with his fellow inmates. Warns the Dutch government about the sale of stolen plutonium and uranium. Transferred to prisons in Haarlem and Leeuwarden. Appointed chairman of the *Association of Foreign Detainees on Dutch territory*. Inhuman treatment and even torture in the prisons seriously undermine his health.

1985 – Appointed under the name O. Milos Voijnovic to editor of the U.S. monthly for Serbian political emigrants *Srpski Glasni* (The Voice of Serbia). Publishes *The Dutch Mafia* (partly confiscated, the rest bought up).

1986 – Writes at the request of among others Ronald Reagan, Henry Kissinger, Bob Dole and Philip Crane a top secret memorandum *How to End the Cold War and Liberate Western Europe from the Communist Yoke*. Memorandum is accepted. Begins issuing forewarnings to various US and foreign authorities of attacks with planes on strategic targets in New York, Washington, London, The Hague, Frankfurt, The Vatican and Mecca. English translation of *Operation Twins* is confiscated by the CIA and the

planned film is abandoned. Released from prison. Deportation to
Yugoslavia and certain death for state treason is prevented at the
last minute by a court injunction, protest from the Red Cross and
Human Rights campaigners and the timely diplomatic interven-
tion by 43 U.S. Congressmen and Senators (see the telex below).

```
mr. c.f korvinus
1017 g amsterdam
prinsengracht 468
(bij de leidsestraat)
amsterdam, the netherlands

dear mr. korvinus:

we, the undersigned, are concerned over the fate of mr. slobodan
mitric should he be forcibly extradited from the netherlands to
yugoslavia.  at the very least, if mr. mitric were returned to
yugoslavia, he would face a life of brutal imprisonment.  more than
likely, he would return to a death sentence.

the district court in the hague, ruling on provisions in the treaty
of rome, has prohibited the netherlands government from expelling
mr. mitric to yugoslavia.  i would urge the appellate court to take

into full consideration the built-in protection against the violation
of human rights as prescribed in the treaty of rome.  the netherlands
government has an excellent record of safeguarding the rights of the
individual.  mr. mitric is counting on receiving due process in the
courts of the netherlands, because he will certainly not be afforded
that basic right in yugoslavia.

in the event that the decision of the district court in the hague
is
overturned, we would ask that mr. mitric be permitted to file a
petition with the european commission of human rights.  during this
time, we will be working to find a host country that will grant mr.
mitric
citizenship and allow him to live in peace and freedom.

once again, we would ask that the decision of the district court in
the hague be upheld.
rep. philip m. crane, r-il.
sen. robert dole, r-kas.
rep. robert michel, r-il.
rep. william broomfield, r-mich.
rep. morris udall, d-ariz.
rep. guy vander jagt, r-mich.
rep. henry hyde, r-il.
rep. robert dornan, r-calif.
rep. dan daniel, d-va.
rep. richard shelby, d-ala.
rep. trent lott, r-miss.
rep. robert lagomarsino, r-cal.
rep. g.v. montgomery, d-miss.
rep. carroll hubbard, d-ky.
rep. gerald solomon, r-n.y.
rep. dan young, r-alaska
rep. charles stenhom, d-tex.
rep. raymond mcgrath, r-n.y.
rep. buddy roemer, d-la.
rep. chalmers wylie, r-ohio
rep. george wortley, r-n.y.
rep. bob stump, r- ariz.
rep. david dreier, r-calif.
rep. bill lowery, r-calif.
rep. william dannemeyer, r-calif.
rep. bill archer, r-tex.
rep. tom loeffler, r-tex.
rep. steve bartlett, r-tex.
rep. thomas hartnett, r-s.c.
rep. william hendon, r-n.c.
rep. jim courter, r-n.j.
rep. helen bentley, r-md.
rep. richard armey, r-tex.
rep. duncan hunter, r-calif.
rep. john kasich, r-ohio
rep. william carney, r-n.y.
rep. james sensenbrenner, r-wis.
rep. robert davis, r-mich.
rep. webb franklin, r-miss.
rep. french slaughter, r-va.
rep. john duncan, r-tenn.
rep. benjamin gilman, r-n.y.
```

1986 (Cont'd) - All subsequent requests for a residence permit in the Netherlands are rejected, till this day he remains an undesirable alien without proper medical attention and pro-active legal assistance and living under the constant threat of being deported in spite of the still valid legal ruling forbidding this.

Receives from the Arizona College of Police Science in absentia an honorary doctorate in law for his trilogy *Operation Twins* (see diploma below) and for his thesis on the new criminological doctrine of *Estherism* (see chapter 13 in this book).

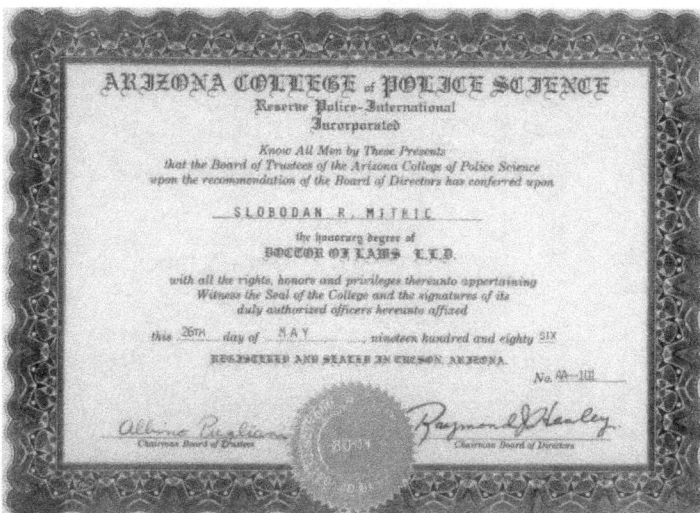

Appointed by Major General Raymond J. Healey as European Director of Reserve Police International (RPI) and of World Atomic Counter-Espionage (WACE) both located in Tucson.

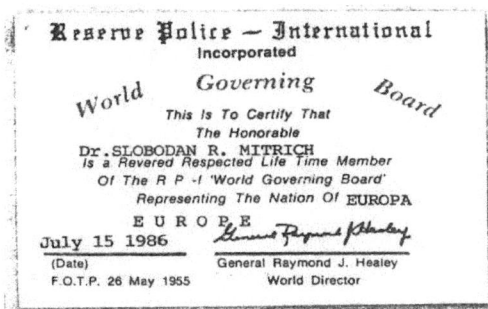

History Corporate Inquiry
File Number: -0508157-5

Corp. Name: RESERVE POLICE INTER-NATIONAL

Domestic Address

4771 S GOLDENROD DR
TUCSON , AZ 85730

Statutory Agent Information

Agent Name: RAYMOND HEALEY

Agent Address:

4771 S GOLDENROD DR

TUCSON, AZ 85730

Agent Status: APPOINTED 03/07/1983

Agent Last Updated:

Additional Corporate Information

Business Type:	**Corporation Type:** NON-PROFIT
Incorporation Date: 10/05/1982	TUAL
Domicile: ARIZONA	**County:** PIMA
Approval Date: 10/12/1982	**Original Publish Date:** 11/12/1982
Status: REVOKED-FILE ANNUAL REPORT	**Status Date:** 03/10/1994

World Leaders Supporting *Reserve Police International.*

First published in the 1983 Spring Issue of THE GLOBE, Tucson, Arizona.

1987 – Foils plans to kidnap and kill Dutch Crown Prince William Alexander by rogue elements within the Dutch secret service. His attempt to also save the life of rich industrialist Gerrit Jan Heijn fails; instead he is arrested and jailed. Describes the gory details in his true crime and love story *The Golden Tip – The Entangle-*

ment of the Upper and Underworld and the Murder of Gerrit Jan Heijn published in English in 2009. Like his previous true crime on the Dutch Mafia and his counter-espionage novel *Operation Twins*, this documented Golden Tip of more than 500 pages is, with one minor exception, also boycotted by the mainstream Dutch media and press. Later, Dutchman Pieter Jan Brugge, producer of the Hollywood B-thriller *The Clearing* (2004), starring Robert Redford and loosely based on the false plot according to which a disgruntled engineer named Ferdi Elsas was solely responsible for this crime, does not respond to emails offering to disclose to him the true background to this infamous kidnapping case for a remake of the real, much more dramatic story.

1988 – Sentenced in a political process, partly held behind closed doors, to 15 months imprisonment for alleged rape after refusing to divulge the names of the murderers of the slain Heijn. Creates with his partner, the independent Dutch artist Iris de Vries a series of paintings and dozens of icons about the Battle of Kosovo in 1389. Appointed chairman of the *Serbian Commission for Human Rights for Benelux and Scandinavia*.

1989 – Publishes a poetic drama *The Battle of Kosovo*. Without a residence or work permit he is reduced to collecting and selling scrap-iron to gain a living; his future wife Iris reduced to picking up thrown-away foodstuff from the market in order to survive.

1990 – Writes, again at the request of the U.S. government, a top secret memorandum *How to Liberate the Yugoslav people from the Communist Yoke*. For the liberation of Serbia, Mitric demands an advance payment of one billion and seven hundred million U.S. dollars. Demand is refused. Starts in Amsterdam a trilingual journal *Srpska Armija/ The Serbian Army / L'armée Serb*.

1991 – Begins with his partner Iris the magazine *L'Atelier de la Liberté* (Laboratory of Freedom) under which name he is later to make many film documentaries.

1992 – Marries Iris de Vries. Refuses an offer from the Dutch government, which had supplied him with a diplomatic passport, to cooperate with a scheme of the Dutch Foreign Intelligence Service (IDB) to liquidate the KGB director in Moscow. Receives a Certificate of Honor from the Free State of Serbia for "Outstanding Service and Contributions to the Struggle for Freedom." Appointed Minister of Defense of the Government-in-Exile of The Free State of Serbia; his wife Iris de Vries refuses to accept her nomination as President of the World Anti-Marxist International.

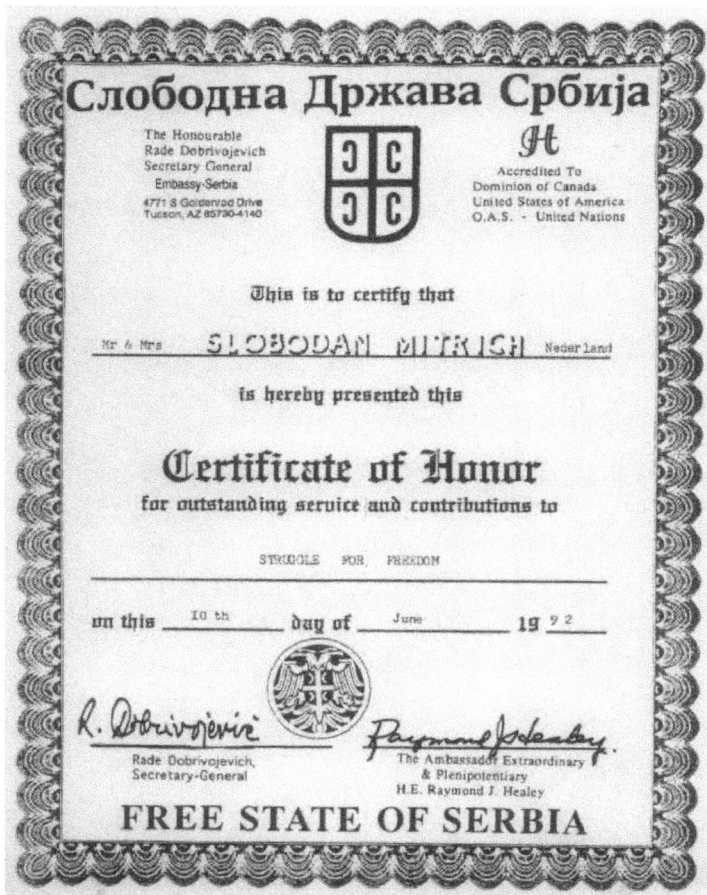

Слободна Држава Србија

The Honourable
Rade Dobrivojevich
Secretary General
Embassy-Serbia
4771 S Goldenrod Drive
Tucson, AZ 85730-4140

Accredited To
Dominion of Canada
United States of America
O.A.S. - United Nations

This is to certify that

Mr & Mrs   SLOBODAN MITRICH   Nederland

is hereby presented this

Certificate of Honor
for outstanding service and contributions to

STRUGGLE FOR FREEDOM

on this ___10 th___ day of ___June___ 19 92

Rade Dobrivojevich,
Secretary-General

The Ambassador Extraordinary
& Plenipotentiary
H.E. Raymond J. Healey

FREE STATE OF SERBIA

1993 – Appointed general director of Reserve Police-International by retired Major General Raymond J. Healey for life, a position he retains and uses also after RPI was subsequently disbanded in the US and refounded by him in a West-European country.

1999 – Publishes *Operacija blizanci* (*Operation Twins*, Part 1) in Serbian in Amsterdam.

2000 – Begins, usually together with his wife Iris, a number of documentary films: including *The Artist Robert Jan Kelder, Amsterdam Jazz, The Shepherd – The Return of Karate Bob, The Director Erik de Vries, Magic Ball Hans Snoek, Erik and Hans, Complaint by Iris de Vries, Hare Krishna, Iris à Paris.*

157

2 5 th September 1993

The Honourable Slobodan Mitrich residing at

2 5 Zeeburgerdijk 1093 SK Amsterdam

Netherlands-Nederland

is hereby named and appointed from this day and date
forward as the ; –

WORLD DIRECTOR

Reserve Police – International

Succeeding Founder / Director Raymond J. Healey (1973)

Given unto my hand and seal

This 25th Day of September 1993

Raymond J.Healey retains the right of Veto power

GEN RAYMOND J HEALEY

Public Hanging For Narco Pushers — Mules & Muleteams

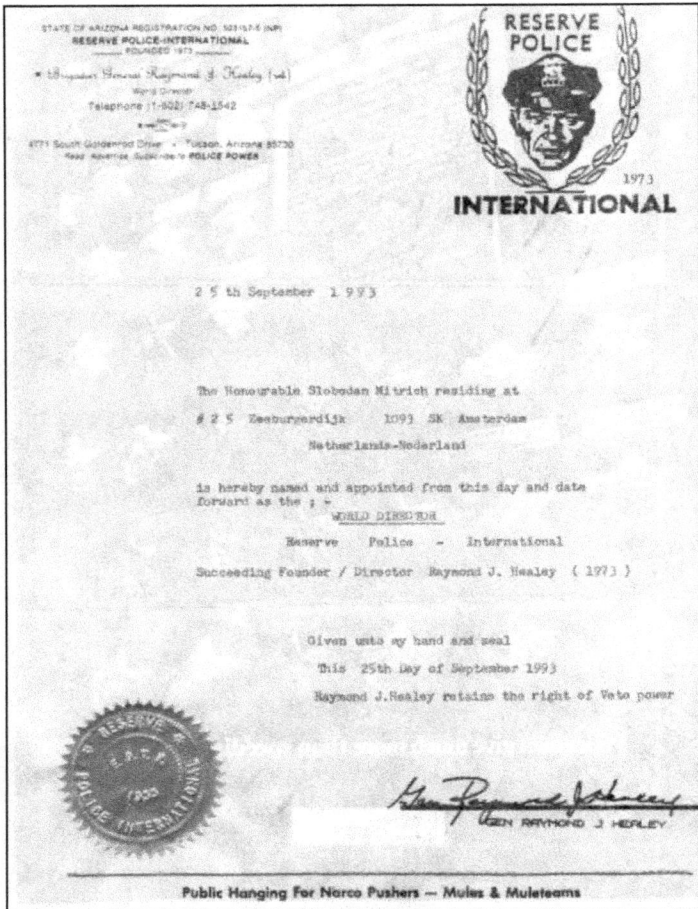

2005 – Publishes a new English translation of *Operation Twins* Part I with many documented appendices on his life and work.

2006 – Publishes new excerpt of *Operation Twins II*. A renewed attempt by the Dutch government to deport him after the death of his wife Iris de Vries on January 10 is again blocked by legal measures and public protests. Edits and publishes an illustrated book *The Boulevard of Bygone Chances* by his late wife.

2007- Publishes a second book *Liberty of the Press* by Iris de Vries.

2008 – Publishes the original Serbian version of *The Golden Tip*.

Later the Dutch version *De Gouden Tip* is published by the Wille-halm Institute Press. Starts writing a new book that "will cause the world to tremble."

2009 – After finishing this novel, publishes 30 hard-cover copies in L'Atelier de la Liberté he makes known the title: *HELP! THEY'VE KIDNAPPED ME! LADY DI.* Describes it as "a modern fairy tale about a princess who is still alive" and dedicates it again to his wife Iris de Vries. Begins with the publisher to translate the novel into Dutch and English.

2010 – The Lady Di Book is presented at the London Book Fair and at BookExpo America. Scottish thriller author Miller Cald-well calls it indeed "A fairytale to rock the Establishment" in his review in the U.K. edition of The London Times for May 22. Draws up a contract with his publisher Robert Jan Kelder for an advanced edition of *9/11: The Accusation – Bringing the Guilty to Justice* and starts writing it. Another attempt on his life, coupled with poor health prompt him at the end of June not to appear in public anymore.

2011 – Publishes the original Serbian version of the 9/11 book *ОПЕРАЦИЈА БЛИЗАНЦИ 9/11 – ТУЖБА* in his L'Atelier de la Liberté. The English translation is slated to be launched at BookExpo America in New York City from May 24-26. An-nounces during the Dutch Book Week in April a new true crime blockbuster *Dead End Street – Why the Dutch Secret Service killed their Top Secret Agent Theo van Gogh,* providing the real background to this famous assassination case. In May he an-nounces a new Serbian book entitled *God's Secrets.*

Appendix XXI – Contract 9/11 – The Accusation

Contract in Dutch and English between
Author and Publisher of *9/11 – The Accusation*
as an advanced edition of *Operation Twins* I and II

CONTRACT VAN DE ROMAN "OPERATION TWINS" TWEEDE EN DERDE DEEL

Tussen auteur Slobodan Radojev Mitric (geb. 1 maart 1948) en
Uitgever Robert Jan Kelder (geb. 29 november 1939).
Beide partijen gaan akkoord dat de romans "OPERATION TWINS" - TWEEDE EN DERDE DEEL
zal bestrijken 400 pagina's.
De uitgever betaalt als voorschot aan de auteur 100.000 euro's (honderdduizend euro's).
De uitgever was niet in staat meteen – ondanks belofte - om de complete roman te financieren. Om dit
geld rond te krijgen heeft de uitgever een tussenoplossing bedacht: beide partijen gaan akkoord dat van
dezelfde roman wordt geschreven een tussenroman "9/11 – De aanklacht". Deze tussenroman zal
hebben 100 pagina's, waarvan de uitgever betaalt 10.000 euro (tienduizend euro's) als voorschot aan
de auteur.
De nettowinst wordt verdeeld:
Naar de auteur 50%
Naar de uitgever 50%

Amsterdam, 10 januari 2010

Getekend op 27 oktober 2010

(Slobodan Radojev Mitric)   (Robert Jan Kelder)

CONTRACT ABOUT THE NOVEL "OPERATION TWINS" SECOND AND THIRD PART
Between de author Slobodan Radojev Mitric (born ,1 March 1948) and
Publisher Robert Jan Kelder (born, 29 November 1939)
Both parties agree that the novels "Operation Twins" – Second and Third Part will have 400 pages.
The publisher pays an advance of 100.000 (hundred thousand) Euro's to the author.
The publisher was not able – in spite of a promise – to finance the complete novel. In order to get this
money, the publisher has come up with a intermediary solution: both parties agree that from the same
novel an intermediary novel will be written "9/11 – The Accusation" .This intermediary novel will
have 100 pages, for which the publisher will pay an advance of 10.000 (ten thousand) Euro's to the
author.
The net profit will be divided:
To the author: 50%
To the publisher 50%

Amsterdam, January 10, 2010

Signed, October 27, 2010

(Slobodan Radojev Mitric)   (Robert Jan Kelder)

Appendix XXII - *The Golden Tip*

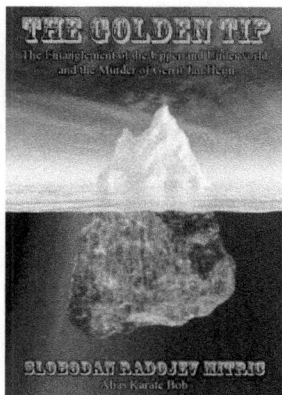

In the fall of 2006, the anthroposophist and publisher Robert Jan Kelder told the author Slobodan Radojev Mitric, known as Karate Bob, in Amsterdam that the widow of rich industrialist Gerrit Jan Heijn had just released an autobiography about the kidnapping and murder of her husband in September 1987. In her book entitled *Reconciliation*, Hank Heijn mentions a brief meeting with a "certain Karate Bob", who claimed to have a "golden tip" about the kidnapping and murder of her husband, but this is dismissed by the widow as nothing more the imagination of this "known killer and rapist".

In his riposte, the author describes hitherto unknown events beginning almost one year before the moment that multimillionaire Gerrit Jan Heijn was abducted. Towards the end of 1986, criminal elements within the Dutch Secret Services were preparing to stage a coup d'état and hire leading members of the underworld to kidnap the Dutch Crown Prince William Alexander and extort 100 million guilders from the Kingdom of The Netherlands. One of the conspirators was an aeronautical-electrical engineer, who had been dismissed from his job…Counter Intelligence from the Dutch Kingdom, together with the assistance of the European director of Reserve Police International operating as private detective Dr. Troublemaker (synonym for the author), succeed in tracking down the conspirators. Brief actions followed another in swift succession in which almost all the conspirators disappear from the face of the earth…

The author has dedicated his true crime and love story of more than 500 pages to his late wife Iris Mitric-de Vries. The richly illustrated book is preceded by an account and appeal by the publisher, an open letter by Slobodan Mitric to the widow of G. J. Heijn plus a summary and list of dramatis personae. It ends with a fourfold afterword and 12 appendices, including a short biography of the author and an open letter to Dutch Queen Beatrix, both containing new facts.

Read this bold and engaging novel with its many narrative layers and hilarious interludes and judge for yourself whether this really is THE GOLDEN TIP.

Willehalm Institute Press, Amsterdam
ISBN 9789073932159
www.willehalm.nl/thegoldentip.htm; http://thegoldentip.blogspot.com

XXIII - "A Fairytale to Rock the Establishment"

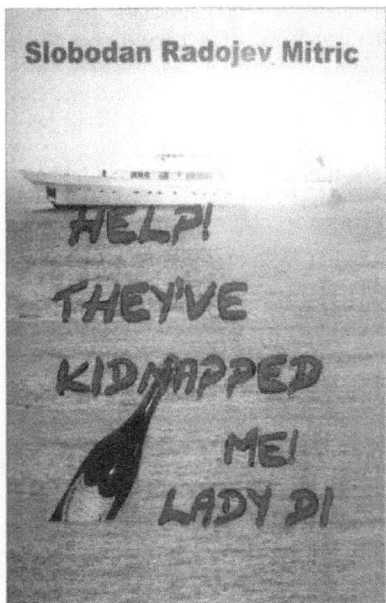

The story takes place between London, Paris, Saint-Tropez, Washington, Amsterdam and the United Arab Emirates in the 80 and 90-ties beginning with the meeting of the young Lady Diana with the twelve years older Prince Charles, their marriage in St. Paul's Cathedral, their love affairs, their painful divorce, and finally Diana's relationship with the Egyptian millionaire and film producer Dodi al-Fayed. This enchanting fairytale complete with a magician and black witch ends with the brutal death of Diana, Dodi and their driver Henri Paul after being chased by paparazzi in the Alma tunnel in Paris. But the book describes how behind the scenes for years a complicated web of competing intrigues was woven around the "princess of the people" with a totally different twist of the story as the baffling outcome.

Like the earlier book *The Golden Tip* by top counter-intelligence agent and criminologist Slobodan Radojev Mitric this multi-level thriller with a touch of eroticism deals with the abduction of a VIP, with the use of doubles, brute force by criminals, corrupt police officers and involved intelligence services like MI5 and MI6. Dedicated to his deceased artist-wife Iris and based on his own experiences and intelligence work, Mitric's book presents a serious argument for starting off were the last inquest into the 'death' of Princes Diana and Dodi al-Fayed ended.

"A Fairytale to Rock the Establishment" Scottish author Miller Caldwell called this true crime novel in his review of May 22, 2010 for the U.K. edition of The London Times.

Willehalm Institute Press, Amsterdam
ISBN 9789073932180
www.willehalm.nl; http://help-ladydi.blogspot.com

Appendix XXIV – *Dead End Street*

Pre-announcement by Slobodan Mitric of a New True Crime On the Real Background to the Murder of Theo van Gogh

<u>Appendix XXV – God's Secrets</u>

Pre-announcement of a New Serbian Novel by Slobodan Mitric

Foreword to *God's Secrets*, a Modern Fairytale

More than 2000 years ago extra-terrestrials visited our planet in order to start an experiment here, "Leave the human being in freedom to perfect himself", which apparently in the eyes of the headquarters of very civilized worlds has now been regarded as an utter failure.

Now twelve gigantic space ships from outer space are heading towards our planet with room for a thousand free seats in each of the ships. Last week, the space ships already passed by the orbit of Pluto. They will become clearly visible for optical telescopes when they approach the orbit of Mars. The ships will reach our planet between December 24 2012 and January 7 2013. That is approximately the date of birth of those who 2000 years ago left our planet in order request the supreme commander of the universe to spare our planetary companions (us) from destruction and to give us a new chance. However, the extra-terrestrials shall not grant us a last chance this time, because for that they have no mandate, their instructions are clear: Destroy all those who directly or indirectly present a threat to the very survival of the planet earth. The one who sent them to punish us, can however at any moment countermand his order, if he becomes convinced that we are finally prepared to leave the paths of self-destruction, because at this moment we are capable of not only destroying the whole human race, but also the animals in nature. And if we refuse to disarm completely, the penal expedition will destroy us collectively with Gobnishud rays that only effect human beings, while the flora and fauna will be completely saved. Before activating the Gobnishud rays, the extra-terrestrials will take in their ships all those whose names are known to headquarters of the universe, in total 12,000 souls; the others will be destroyed. They have only come to save the chosen ones, but the Gobnishud rays can also be emitted from the capital of the Gobnishud cosmic state. Do not think that this time we can avoid our punishment, no matter what function we have in this vampire world.

But we still have more than a year to greet the extra-terrestrials with courtesy, and to show them we find it worthwhile to live. Do we find it worthwhile to live? It seems to me that we do. And if we do not, a new generation of human beings will come forth from the ones already chosen who are capable of doing this.

This is not the first time in the history of our planet that the supreme commander of the universe does something like that. If we do not come to our senses in time, the universe loses nothing, and we a lot. Why not support this last chance for salvation, for the complete rescue. Let us prove that we truly find living life worthwhile. Should we allow 6 billion souls on this planet to be destroyed for the sake of the egoism of a handful of our planetary companions, who think that they are Gods, while they are not even worthy of being called human beings?

Gobnishud

"A well devised , contemporary theme (...) The term 'planetary companions' is a great find. Go on, keep at it."

Rade Bozovic

* 9 7 8 9 0 7 3 9 3 2 0 0 5 *